What Others ar
Groundings S

A consummate story teller, and a teacher who walks her talk, I can think of no one better to bring this kind of book to the church. When our church needed a pastor to take us out of the pew and into the neighborhood; to focus less on ourselves and more on the voice of Jesus, we turned to Candie Blankman. More than a curriculum, *Groundings* is a guide book for discipleship that teaches you to listen deeply to Jesus and then plunges you deeply into the lives of the people all around you every day. I would urge every pastor to buy a copy—or 12—and use it to reignite a movement of discipleship in your congregation.

Tod Bolsinger, Vice President, and Chief of Leadership Formation, Fuller Seminary, author of *Canoeing the Mountains: Christian Leadership in Uncharted Territory.*

All pastors desire to see Christ's transforming power at work in the lives of the members of their church. As we utilized *Groundings* in our church, I was able to witness firsthand the change in participants' lives as they met together in small groups, discussed the scriptures, and listened to the Spirit speaking to them in new ways through familiar stories. *Groundings* pushes participants beyond just knowledge to a new way of living as Christ-followers. It challenges people to participate in what God is already doing in their lives and in the lives of co-workers, friends, and neighbors.

Steve Schibsted
Pastor, First Presbyterian Church of Berkeley

Do you remember hearing this phrase, "He/She is so heavenly minded they are of no earthly good?" Candie Blankman's book helps us see the heavenly minded teachings of Jesus firmly grounded in a personal lifestyle that is not only good, but earth-shaking good. *Groundings* is way beyond the usual discipleship curriculum. The fascinating stories take you from the front porch to half way around the world showing the power of discipleship in action. As you read, you will think of specific moments, people, and exciting opportunities to engage a diverse culture with life-changing effectiveness. I am personally going to use *Groundings* to teach discipleship in a fresh way. But first I must talk with a friend I thought of while reading. I need to hear his story and share my own. That kind of inspiration is the unique power of *Groundings.*

Ken Davis
Award winning author of 12 books, motivational and inspirational speaker, President of Ken Davis Productions and Lighten Up Ministries.

Groundings Stories

Groundings Stories

Continuing the Work of Jesus in the World

Candie Blankman

Bold Vision Books
PO Box 2011
Friendswood, Texas 77549

ISBN 9781946708151

Author photo by Ali Bolsinger of www.alibeephotos.com
Cover Art © Everst | Dreamstime.com
Cover Design by Maddie Scott
Interior by kae Creative Solutions

Published by Bold Vision Books, PO Box 2011,
Friendswood, Texas 77569

Published in the United States of America.

Table of Contents

Acknowledgments

I am especially thankful to my congregation, San Clemente Presbyterian Church, that provided much of the platform for developing *Groundings.* I am grateful for two pastors and colleagues, Steve Wright and Craig Williams, who sat down with me at the very beginning to brainstorm and flesh out my ideas. I am thankful to the more than one hundred people at San Clemente Presbyterian who entrusted their sacred lives of faith to this experience. I am especially thankful to Sheryl France-Moran, a coworker and beloved friend at San Clemente Presbyterian Church, and one of the first students who enthusiastically embraced and lived out *Groundings* and is now teaching the experience to others. In addition, as Mission Participation Director she has worked with me to incorporate the *Groundings* principles in the orientation and execution of all our mission teams. It has made a difference in the way these teams approach going into the world.

I am thankful for my husband Drew who always provides the space and support for me to pursue whatever it is I believe God is calling me to do. Even if it means being on his own foraging for food in the refrigerator, or my absence for days and weeks at a time, seeing me up late at night, up early in the morning, and sometimes, up all night; he cheers me on with a steady, "Go for it Candie, but pace yourself." I always need both the encouragement and the caution.

Finally, I am thankful to the Lord for all of the grace and patience extended to me on this journey to follow Him and drag others along with me. A poor and very ordinary young girl, I have had the rich privilege of serving Christ in extraordinary places and times in extraordinary ways. And because it has helped me to see the extraordinary work of God in ordinary places, I consider the *Groundings* experience to be one of the richest privileges of all. To God be the glory.

Introduction

In the winter of 2014 when I led the first *Groundings* experience, I remember standing in front of the group during the second session trembling. I was not sure if I would be able to hold it together. I had developed the curriculum over a period of several months and carefully chosen the biblical narratives that I believed would most powerfully demonstrate the basic principles of what it meant to follow Jesus—to be a true disciple. I called it *Groundings* because we all need to be rooted and grounded in Christ. But, these were not intellectual principles. They were principles that could only be lived out in real life. They could not simply be understood. To understand them was to practice them. I confess I had never practiced them quite like this before.

After studying and preparing and doing the assignment for the second *Groundings* session, I was completely humbled by what I was coming to understand. I had chosen the biblical narratives because I thought they demonstrated the basic principles of discipleship as demonstrated by Jesus himself. I had not realized until I started teaching and studying them together with these people that there was another principle demonstrated by these stories that was not in the original plan for the curriculum. Every one of the stories, all of them, clearly revealed how clueless the religious leaders were at the time when Jesus was teaching. In every story, without fail, it was the religious leaders, those educated in the scriptures, the law, the Torah, the teachers, the scribes and Pharisees who the stories revealed as unable and unwilling to receive what Jesus had to say. In fact, in most cases, they were in direct opposition, at times hostile to what Jesus was teaching.

I stood trembling in front of this first *Groundings* experience group because I feared that I might be one of them—one of the clueless, educated, religious leaders who was unable or unwilling to receive what Jesus was teaching. It is so easy to read the Bible and see how stiff-necked and arrogant the Israelites or Pharisees were. It is easy even today to look out across the church and identify people who seem to be oblivious to the radical life Jesus calls us to. But to examine myself, my own blindness? Almost impossible. I trembled because I was afraid I was one of them. Full of education, full of knowledge, working for God my whole life, and yet, like the Pharisees and the disciples in these narratives, was I missing what Jesus was doing and teaching? I had recently witnessed up close and personal many self-proclaimed followers of Jesus saying and doing unbelievably unbiblical and un-Jesus like things, all in the name of love of Christ and devotion to the Scripture. How could they be so blind? Was I blind, too?

The opposite revelation in these stories was also transforming for me. It was the sinners, the outsiders, the shunned and marginalized in Jesus' time who came to Him and understood Him and followed Him eagerly. It was not the exception it was the rule. Simeon was disgusted by the woman who anointed Jesus' feet. Jesus said her story would be proclaimed wherever the Good News was preached. The disciples could not imagine why Jesus was talking to a Samaritan woman at the well and yet it was she that brought a crowd to hear Jesus. The priest and the Levite were teachers who passed by the victim by the side of the road, but the despised Samaritan showed costly compassion, allowing his life to be seriously interrupted. Jesus affirmed him, and he was the one Jesus used to teach others in this parable. The disciples along with the whole community despised Zacchaeus, yet Zacchaeus immediately responded to Jesus and was transformed with a radically generous new way of life. Jesus makes Zacchaeus the example of what it means to be a son of Abraham, a follower of Jesus. And finally, Nicodemus, a leader of the Jews came by night to ask Jesus questions, but did he really want to learn? Jesus challenged him. How could he be a teacher of Israel and yet not know these things about being born of the Spirit?

Groundings changed me. I no longer assume because I am a pastor and employed by the church and have a Master of Divinity degree (whoever came up with that title?) that I can be sure I am on the right track in following Jesus. Every person has a risk of blindness to the radical teaching of Jesus. Every time we open the Bible to read about the Jesus we say we follow, we need to be prepared to be confronted anew with a living Christ who has asked us to deny ourselves and take up our cross and follow Him...into the world.

Groundings has reawakened my desire for God by following Jesus more carefully and more closely whatever the cost. After years of education and years of studying and preaching and teaching the Bible, I am once again authentically a student at the feet of Jesus.

What follows are *Groundings* stories. The names and some of the circumstances have been changed in all of these *Groundings* stories, but the stories are of real people who through *Groundings* have learned how to notice and follow the living and powerful Christ every day. They have been awakened to God at work in the world all around them all the time. They have been and are being transformed. Their stories continue to inspire me. I know you, too, will be inspired by these stories. I hope you will experience *Groundings.* And, I pray the Lord will use it to transform your life, too and renew the spiritual life of His church.

Candie Blankman

God in a Birdbath

I met her on the church patio. Lilly was visiting relatives and came to church with them on this Sunday morning. I quickly learned she was unchurched due largely to her family of origin. Consequently, I was very interested in how she experienced our worship service. She had a lot of good things to say about her experience but said the sermon was "preachy." Hmmmm. This one I would have to chew on awhile since we churchy types call it preaching. The critique is worth an extended conversation with other preachers. And, it also merits further inquiry with other infrequent church goers.

The longer I spoke with Lilly the more I realized how different her experience was from mine. I was in church at four days old, and when I was growing up we were in church whenever the church doors were open, which meant at least three times a week. Sunday morning worship, Sunday night Bible study and Wednesday night prayer meeting were all priorities in our family schedule. And unlike the experience of some, I never left the church—not in high school, not in college, not after I got married. And now, I have been employed by the church for twenty-five of the last thirty-two years. I have attended worship and been active in church my entire life. Without revealing how old I am, let's just say it is many years.

Though Lilly's mother had been raised Methodist, her father was an outspoken atheist. He forbade Lilly's mother to take her and her brother to church with the exception of an occasional holiday service. Lilly had occasionally visited church with high school and college friends. But for the most part, it was foreign territory for her. She told me that her main contact with church as an adult was funerals. Wow! That would give a different spin to a person's experience of church. I was fascinated by this difference and wondered how I might learn from her. After all, Jesus made it clear early on in His ministry that He came for those outside of the sheepfold (John 10:26).

Lilly lived in another state and returned home shortly after our conversation. Secretly I wished Lilly lived closer so that I could talk to her and learn more about what it was like to be raised and live life so unconnected to a church. Though she was off my visual radar Lilly kept coming up in my thoughts and prayers. The *Groundings* teacher was staring a *Groundings* experience square in the face, but the geography and proximity impaired my vision.

A couple of months later I was the speaker for the confirmation retreat for our church. One of the regular components of the weekend is called, "Ask the Pastor." During this time around a campfire, the confirmation students can ask the pastor any question they want. Yes. Any question they want. This is a space I entered with fear and trembling. I was a junior high public school teacher before I entered full-time ministry. I knew well the potential of their creative and mischievous minds. But all was well. Their questions varied from the sublime to the ridiculous.

Nothing was asked that caught me completely by surprise. One boy did ask a question that I simply could not answer at all. He asked me when and why I stopped going to church. At first, because of my total lack of a personal frame of reference, I did not understand the question. After questioning him a little, I realized what he was asking. The young man was wondering how old I was when my parents quit making me go to church. Good question since it was likely that all of these young people were attending church because their parents insisted. They were now being asked to make a commitment on their own to follow in the footsteps of Jesus and to be a faithful participant in the life of our church. Though they were all cooperating to varying degrees in their participation in the life of the church, it is unlikely that any of them could have chosen at the time to stop attending altogether. I knew my response would be unsatisfying for this inquiring young mind and heart. I could only answer his question by saying that I never did stop going to church. I explained to the confirmation students that I had never been away from the church or turned away from my faith. Dead silence followed.

This question immediately brought Lilly to mind. I realized again that my understanding of church was in some way lacking because I had never been away from it. How could I know what that absence was like? How could I know what life was like for a person who had little or no experience of church? How could I understand the people who were unchurched when my whole life was church centered? How could I minister to people outside the church if I had no idea what it was like to be outside the church? Lilly was the answer. She could help me understand what it was like to be "outside" of the church and what it felt like to visit or to be a newcomer. I decided that when I returned from the retreat I would give her a call and ask her to teach me.

Well, as often is the case with "come down from the mountain" camp experiences, I was less sure of this idea when I got back to my church office the next week. My mind was busy imagining all the possible reactions she might have to my calling her. What would she think? I hardly knew her. I was a pastor and she had been out of church her whole life. I would probably just annoy her. Or, I might offend her by even asking. I decided to play it safe. I would email her first and give her the opportunity to easily decline or just ignore my email. I discovered that even sending the email was hard for me to do.

These feelings show how difficult it can be for churched people to interact with unchurched people. It's as if we are from another country and speak a different language. It is like going to an event where you don't know anyone and you have no idea what you are supposed to do, or not do, say or not say. It is a place of great vulnerability where the newcomer has little control. And we all know how important control is. I realized this out-of-control feeling is what it must be like for people to attend a worship service or other church events when they have not been raised in the environment. They are visiting a foreign country that uses a foreign language. There is much to learn here about how we can do church in a way that softens the foreignness of this experience for outsiders who come in.

I decided that it might seem less intrusive to Lilly if I told her about the question that I was asked on the confirmation retreat. I would be totally transparent and tell her that my purpose in talking with her was to help me learn and perhaps respond more thoughtfully and intelligently to this kind of question from the young people of my church. Perhaps talking to her and hearing her story would help me be better prepared next time. I typed the email and then sat with my finger poised over the send key for at least a minute. Then I put my hand down. I wasn't going to do it. This was stupid. Lilly didn't want to talk to a pastor about her experience of life outside of the church. She barely knew me, and I lived far away. For at least five minutes, I vigorously debated with myself using all the reasons for and against contacting her. Finally, the debate ended. My conscience as the creator and facilitator of the *Groundings* experience compelled me to take the risk. I knew that I had to practice what

I was teaching in *Groundings*. I needed to be open to the conversation no matter where it led or even if it led nowhere. I said a prayer, raised my finger over the send button again and, this time, I pressed it. It was done. Now I would wait.

To my great surprise and delight, Lilly replied to my email the same day. She said that she would be glad to have some conversation with me. She went further. Lilly said that my email "made her day." She was not offended. She was not annoyed. She did not experience my inquiry as intrusive. Lilly explained that she had been wanting to talk to someone about her spiritual experiences for a long time and that she was grateful for my interest and willingness to talk to her. My unfounded hesitation was a good lesson for insiders about reaching people outside the church. Holy cow! How wrong I was. How self-centered I was. I was more concerned about what she would think about me than I was about her. I was more concerned about personal rejection than I was about learning to be a better disciple and learning to proclaim the good news of the gospel to outsiders. Sending that email was a game changer for me. Lilly and I agreed on a time to connect by phone in the next couple of weeks. This was a *Groundings* experience if there ever was one. But this is just the beginning of this story.

My subsequent conversations with Lilly revealed the most remarkable evidence of God at work in her life from the very beginning. Her father's ban on going to church did not prevent the Lord from entering into her life. God's relentless searching love is not confined to houses of worship or religious institutions. God by

His Spirit and through circumstances and His people is active in every square inch of the universe and can use the most unexpected spaces and times and people.

Lilly's mother had passed away twenty years ago. But she had a story from her early childhood that is beyond amazing. Lilly had never told this story to anyone outside the family. I knew when she told it to me that I had entered sacred space. The phone conversation with Lilly now became a third space. It was not just two people on the phone. It was two people on the phone with the Lord God Almighty hosting the conversation.

Lilly's father had forbidden her mother to take her brother and her to church. But that did not stop her mother from trying to give her children a faith experience. Lilly described an event when Lilly was about three or four years old. She remembered her mother taking her and her brother into a wooded park. Her mother's uncle was a Methodist minister, and he came with them on this outing. Lilly and her brother thought this was strange. They wondered why he was along. After hiking quite a ways into the woods, there in the wooded park was a bird bath. There was no one else around. Only the trees and sky and unseen forest critters were present to bear witness to what was about to happen. There in that birdbath, in the middle of a forest, Lilly's great uncle baptized her and her brother.

I was speechless.

Lilly broke the silence. In a voice that was filled with both hope and fear she asked me, "Does that count?"

This was certainly sacred space. I was hearing sacred things about the way God reaches into the lives of people no matter what their circumstances. No power of an earthly father could ever prevent the love of the heavenly father from breaking through and claiming His own.

I responded without hesitation, "Does that count? Does that count? Of course, that counts," I responded with so much awe and wonder, I thought I would explode. I continued, "This is one of the most amazing baptism stories I have ever heard. I am so honored that you would tell me this story." Then I said, "Thank you," over and over again. These early childhood baptism experiences are confirmed later in life when the person can express personal faith in Christ. Whether infant, child, or adult, all baptisms are only outward signs of inward realities of a regenerative work only the Spirit of God can do.

This birdbath story was one of many stories Lilly told me about her life outside of church. It was a life without church. It was not a life without God. If I had not contacted her I would never have heard this amazing story. Or what if I had approached her as if I was the one to tell her the story and not to listen to hers? What if I had assumed as so much of my early Christian education had instilled in me that because Lilly had not been in church much, not much of God could be in Lilly?

I am so grateful for the example of Jesus in the gospels. In story after story, parable after parable, Jesus encountered people in all sorts of places who were disassociated from the religious people and institutions of the day. Jesus went even further. By association, He affirmed the actions of a woman that His disciples and religious leaders dismissed as a person too sinful to be touching Him (Luke 7:39). And in another gospel, Jesus went beyond mere association and described this woman or another woman similar in circumstances.[1] Either way, Jesus enthusiastically proclaimed that the story would be told by people throughout the world wherever the Gospel was preached (Matthew 26:6-13). Two thousand years later the untouchable woman's story is being told.

Jesus affirmed a woman at a well. The towns people had shunned her and the disciples believed Jesus should not be talking to her. Yet, it was this shunned woman who declared Him as promised Messiah and brought an entire village to hear Jesus. In stark contrast, when the disciples came back from the same village, all they brought with them was lunch. They did not bring a single person to hear Jesus. Her story is also being told two thousand years later (John 4) over and over again. Noticing God at work in the lives of these outsiders and yet extraordinary women opened my heart and mind to realizing that Jesus is alive and at work in every person's life. The only difference is whether we notice it or not.

Lilly was not an outcast or shunned woman. But she was a person on the "outside" when it came to church. Jesus was interested and involved with people on the outside of the synagogue. By the Spirit of God, whom Jesus sent into the world, Jesus continues to be very interested in and involved with people outside the church.

Archbishop Rowan Williams writes that "every object or person we encounter is in a relationship with God before they're in a relationship of any kind with us. And if that doesn't make us approach the world and other people with reverence and amazement, I don't know what will."[2] I will never again look at a birdbath the same way. I will never look at anyone outside the church the same.

I continue to learn from Lilly's story. And the story God is writing in her life is not finished. Noticing God at work and offering ourselves as assistants to that work does not necessarily mean that we will see the conclusion to the story, at least not in this life. Noticing God at work and offering ourselves and the spaces we enter as places and times where God can do kingdom work means that we might be just a small part of a much larger work God is doing. This is wholehearted discipleship. But it always means we give God the credit and the glory for all that He does in us and through us and in others. The whole earth is full of His glory (Isaiah 6:3). Even a birdbath tucked in the woods of a forest preserve can become an altar for His presence and power. A birdbath becomes a third space to proclaim the Kingdom of God. Who knew?

Where can I go from your Spirit?
Where can I flee from your presence?
If I go up to the heavens, you are there;
if I make my bed in the depths, you are there.

If I rise on the wings of the dawn,
if I settle on the far side of the sea,
even there your hand will guide me,
your right hand will hold me fast.
Psalm. 139:7-10

Curbside for Kingdom

Joan had lived in the same neighborhood for more than thirty-five years. For at least the last fifteen years, she observed a man, always alone, taking his garbage container out to end of his driveway as he placed it by the curb. Once in a while, she saw him walking down the street past her house—always by himself. Often Joan would be getting into her car in the morning about the time he headed down his driveway. Sometimes she would wave. He waved back. Other times she pulled into her driveway in the afternoon when she returned from work when he would be walking up the driveway returning his garbage container to its place along the side of the house behind the wooden gate. Joan wondered if he was not married or if he had a wife that was sick.

Joan knew what it was like to care for a sick spouse. Her husband had been bedridden for many years and then had to be placed in a care facility. Her interest was much more than curiosity. She felt deep empathy for the man. But she had never spoken to him and never heard him say a word and didn't know his name. She never took the time to stop and talk. And, to be honest, she really didn't want to talk to him. The high value placed on personal privacy reigns supreme in most American neighborhoods. Eighty-five percent of Americans consider not being disturbed at home important or very important. [3]

After two *Groundings* sessions and two different stories about Jesus encountering people, Joan saw this man differently. Though not laying injured by the side of the road like the man in the story of the Good Samaritan (Luke 10), something about this man seemed wounded. The Good Samaritan allowed his routine to be seriously interrupted in order to help a complete stranger. Joan didn't like it but couldn't shake the idea that the Lord might be nudging her to allow her routine to be interrupted for this neighbor. And because of a fresh look at the story of Zacchaeus in the *Groundings* experience, Joan had learned that everyday places and spaces took on much greater significance. Any space could have significance if Jesus was in it. Luke 19:1-10 records the story of Zacchaeus. Though Jesus invited himself, and though it was the home of Zacchaeus, Jesus was actually the host. Zacchaeus fed the Lord and likely His disciples a meal, but Jesus fed them all living bread. Zacchaeus' house became a third space—a space used by God for eternal purposes. Joan knew that any person could be her neighbor according to the story Jesus told about the Good Samaritan, and she also knew that any space could be used by God for hospitality—used for the Lord to be the host. But never before had she thought about her driveway or the neighbor's driveway or the garbage by the curb or the sidewalk in front of her home as such a place.

Joan had seen Jesus enter everyday spaces and transform those spaces into a space for spiritual conversation. Joan had observed how Jesus took the time to be interrupted to interact with people. Joan realized now that her driveway, the space by the curb with her neighbor's garbage receptacle, and the sidewalk were all *third spaces*—everyday places that God was present and at work. Joan was paying attention and knew that God might be inviting her to enter this space with new eyes and an open heart of spiritual curiosity. She had always assumed and practiced the new Golden Rule—do not bother others and they will not bother you. Joan was sure this neighbor did not want to be bothered, and she didn't want to be bothered. But now with her heart awakened to God at work in every space all the time and with Jesus' very clear teaching that anyone can be our neighbor, Joan knew she had to try and talk to this man who lived three houses down the street.

Joan was nervous and did not know what she would say or how he would respond but she began to pray for an opportunity to cross paths with this neighbor. One morning just as Joan was taking her garbage out to the curb, this man turned onto the sidewalk to begin a morning walk. Joan's heart began beating rapidly and hard. She was sure he would hear it when he got closer. She could think of one hundred reasons why she could not or should not talk to this man, and her brain was signaling every muscle in her body to run back up her driveway to the safety of her own house. But the power of the living Christ revealed in the Bible had captured her attention and was signaling a different response. She said a quick prayer asking God to help her stay put, not be afraid, and to have the right words to say. Then, there he was—right in front of her.

She said, "Good morning." Her mouth was so dry she thought her tongue was stuck and she would not be able to say another word.

"Good morning," he replied, "How are you?"

Now there was no turning back. "I am fine," Joan responded. Her mouth still dry but her tongue loosened a bit, "How are you?" she returned.

"Oh," the man said, "Not very good. My wife died last week after a long battle with cancer. I did not want her to suffer any longer, but it is hard to be alone after so many years."

Joan could not believe what happened next. She said, "I am so sorry for your loss," and then she did not have to say another word. The man talked and she listened for twenty or thirty minutes. He spoke about his wife and losing her. Joan was so in awe of this moment, this space, and what was happening that she lost all track of time. This was a real neighbor, but this was no sidewalk or garbage container space. This was a sacred space where the living Christ was hosting a holy conversation. The garbage was being recycled for kingdom purposes.

When he was done he said, "Thank you for listening."

Joan did not launch into an explanation of the spiritual meaning of death and loss or immediately lead him into saying a prayer to accept Jesus as his Savior.

She realized she still did not know his name. First things first. So, she introduced herself and found out his name was Bill. Joan knew she could do little to console or comfort this man. But she knew what she could do. She said, "I will pray for you, Bill." He looked surprisingly comforted and said, "Thank you," and continued down the sidewalk.

Joan headed back up her driveway and was stunned. It had taken her thirty plus years to talk to her neighbor. Why was she was so hesitant? A simple "How are you?" opened his life up to her, and the sidewalk became a *third space* where God hosted a conversation about death and loss and a sprinkle of hope in the form of an offer to pray. Clearly, God had already been at work in this man through his life and loss. Joan was late to the party. Who knows how many times she had missed invitations to see what God was doing and to enter the space God was working in and to be a part of it? This time she paid attention and had the sacred privilege of entering the *third space* and being a small part of what God was doing in that space.

Why are we so hesitant and timid about talking to people about the Lord and our faith? There are many reasons but every person in the *Groundings* experiences expresses three primary obstacles.

The first obstacle is our selectiveness in our human interaction. We are choosy about who we talk to. We have come to value privacy and fear for our own safety to such an extent that we often purposely avoid talking to people we do not know. Unlike the Good Samaritan's neighbor, our "neighbors" are a select group of people we have chosen to know. Often the people we have chosen to know and treat as neighbors do not even live near us. And many of us, like Joan, have consciously chosen not to know people who are near to us. Being a disciple of Jesus means, like the Good Samaritan story, anybody that God is calling us to love can be a neighbor. In fact, the story goes a step further. The religious passers-by did not see the man in the ditch as a neighbor, and they did not act like a neighbor. The despised Samaritan did both. He *saw* the left-to-die man as a neighbor, and he *acted* as a neighbor to the man. The religious leaders of the day were stunned. It was a double whammy object lesson for those who had ears to hear.

The second obstacle to our openly having conversations about faith is the narrow way we look at our surroundings. We view most spaces from a very self-centered and utilitarian mindset. We limit our view of our spaces to what we normally use those spaces for. The driveway is to drive the car in and out of our garages. The sidewalk is to walk on. The curbside is for putting our garbage out to be collected or a place to park our cars. If we believe that Christ is alive and powerful and active in the world and if we say that we want to be His disciple, to follow Him then means that we see every space we enter differently. We need to see every space as a place where God is at work in some way for His purposes. Any space can become a place where Jesus Christ becomes the host of a conversation or uses us to enter into the life of another. Every one of these experiences can have eternal consequences. Being a disciple, following Jesus means we are open and available to the invitation to join with Him in some way in whatever that work is in whatever space we are in.

A third obstacle is the misconception that we must finish or bring to a conclusion every spiritual conversation we begin or enter. This misconception is the result of failing to understand that God in Christ is at work reconciling the world to himself twenty-four-seven. Colossians 1:20 and 2 Corinthians 5:19, not to mention John 3:16 all reveal God's reconciling work past, present, and future. God in Christ is reconciling the world to himself by means of the cross and as God goes about doing that reconciliation, He invites His disciples, His followers, His hands and feet in the world to join Him in part of that reconciling work. Jesus explains clearly in John 4:34-38 that God is always working and uses different people at different times to do various parts of His work. As proclaimers of the Kingdom of God, we do not have to present, explain, and sign and seal the deal every time.

Joan is not alone in her neighborhood isolation. The priest and the Levite in Luke 10 both had their own fears and concerns related to the Law that made them isolated from the man lying almost dead by the side of the road. The new Golden Rule and the high value placed on personal privacy is like the Law in Luke 10. It has most of us avoiding conversations and shying away from developing relationships with people all around us. And it is not only introverts who behave this way. Extroverts are also often highly selective about connecting with others. This isolation is further exacerbated by the fear that currently grips our hearts and minds because of a deep sense of danger created by all the access to news of violence all around the world. Access to the internet and mobile devices mean we can be engrossed in this fear producing news twenty-four hours a day, seven days a week. If God is truly in control and the Lord of the universe, then God can still work in and through all the spaces and places and people in the world no matter how challenging or tragic or frightening the circumstances.

Following Jesus means we must get our eyes off all the screens and on to people and world around us, and tune our hearts to listen closely for the Spirit of God prompting us to go beyond our fears and trust that same Spirit to guide and protect us. Following Jesus means knowing anyone we encounter can be a neighbor that we need to listen to, and, further, we may be called on to be neighborly toward them. Following Jesus means realizing that every square inch of the universe belongs to God and every space can be a place where Jesus, now alive in us, can be the host offering spiritual food for all those who are open to receiving it. When we understand space as belonging to the Lord we are invited to see all kinds of people in those spaces as our neighbors. And, like the Good Samaritan, we are invited to be like a neighbor to all kinds of unique and different people in those spaces.

You have heard that it was said, "Love your neighbor[i] and hate your enemy." But I tell you, love your enemies and pray for those who persecute you, that you may be children of your Father in heaven. He causes His sun to rise on the evil and the good, and sends rain on the righteous and the unrighteous.
Matthew 5:43-45

Tenderness in a Train Station

In 2014 a local news article caught Andrea's eye. It reported the tragic death of a man who was gunned down by a militant group while traveling overseas. The picture accompanying the article jolted Andrea. Though she did not recognize the man, the woman that he was standing with looked very familiar to her. Dancer thin and model attractive, Andrea quickly recognized the woman in the picture as a mom who had volunteered with her a decade or more earlier in one of Andrea's boy's school groups. Reserved and quiet, but tall and statuesque, Andrea had noticed her before. But now Andrea's heart went out to this woman caught in such a terrible tragedy.

Reading the article confirmed that this male victim of random, possibly extremist violence was the partner and fiancée of the woman Andrea had volunteered alongside years ago. Andrea could not even imagine how awful and complicated and shocking this must have been for this woman. Andrea felt like she should go to her but had no idea how or where. And there was an unapproachable quality to the depth of this tragedy. Andrea felt uncomfortable. In such a fragile and tragic time, she did not want to invade her privacy. But Andrea could not get the image or this woman out of her mind.

When only days later Andrea saw her at the train station, she knew it could not be a coincidence. Andrea was participating in *Groundings,* and she knew that God was constantly working in the world and constantly inviting others to work with Him. Andrea was at the train station to drop off her son who attended a private school in another community. She did not realize this woman's daughter rode the same train and attended the same school. Andrea noticed because she saw a young girl on the train platform drop to her knees weeping. Suddenly this same woman she recognized in the photo in the newspaper article came running from out of her car still in her pajamas. She lifted this young girl, who must have been her daughter, up off of her knees and into her arms. She held her tightly while the train came and went, leaving them alone on the platform. Andrea so wanted to help in some way, but once again felt the nature of this encounter was so intimate she dared not intrude. The woman and her daughter just knelt there embracing, weeping for a long time. Andrea lost track of the time. She watched from her car, riveted, and wanting to do something, but again, Andrea did not feel like it was the right time to approach this grieving woman. As far as Andrea could tell, the woman and her daughter never exchanged a word.

Finally, as the weeping subsided, they returned to the car and, Andrea presumed, the safety of their home. Days and weeks went by. Andrea still could not get this woman out of her mind. She prayed for her each time she thought about her.

Perhaps a month or two later, while attending a choral performance at her son's school, Andrea ran into this same woman in the restroom. Andrea was terribly nervous but she knew, this time, that she had to seize the opportunity to speak to her before she lost her nerve. In such small quarters, it was hard not to acknowledge her. Andrea approached her and gently touched her on the arm and introduced herself. The woman reciprocated the gesture, touching Andrea's hand on her arm and said that her name was Tanya. Tanya immediately remembered and referenced the same volunteer work they had done together many years earlier. Andrea told Tanya that she had been thinking about her, and praying for her. Further, Andrea explained that she had seen her that day on the train station platform. She told her how much she admired and was moved by Tanya's immediate response to her distraught daughter. Andrea told her how terribly sorry she was for her loss. The conversation was surprisingly easy and Tanya seemed equally surprised and grateful for the conversation and responded warmly.

Emboldened by Tanya's warm reception of her, Andrea asked how she was doing. Tanya described the agony of her loss and the struggle to go on day after day but acknowledged that her daughter helped her a lot. Tanya knew she had to go on and be strong for her daughter. It took Andrea by surprise when Tanya thanked her for asking because Andrea had been so sure that asking Tanya how she was doing would be intrusive. They both had places to be so there was little time to talk. As they exchanged good-byes, Andrea reached out and Tanya reciprocated. They held each other briefly. It was a sacred moment, indeed. Andrea was so glad that she had finally spoken with her. More confident now, Andrea wished that there had been more time to listen to her story.

One evening not long after their brief conversation in the restroom, while seriously reflecting on this encounter with Tanya, Andrea suddenly remembered that this woman owned a local business. Andrea decided to stop by the store to see how Tanya was doing. When she did, she discovered the business had been closed. Connecting again seemed impossible. Our attempts and offering ourselves do not always result in an encounter that we can clearly identify as God at work. Sometimes the opportunity does not materialize and nothing happens. Andrea hoped they would somehow meet again. Andrea saw her again at school. This time Tanya was talking and laughing with friends. Andrea did not have any further opportunity to have any conversation with Tanya. But it made Andrea so happy to see her smiling and laughing.

There are souls, situations that nudge you, call to you. For Andrea, Tanya's tragedy was one of them. Andrea learned so much from this encounter even though it unfolded very slowly over several months. The "encounter" really began years before the tragedy occurred when they first encountered each other as mom's helping out at school. Andrea is now trying to respond more quickly to that call and gentle nudge when it comes. At first, Andrea thought this encounter was a failed *Groundings* moment. It was not. It simply took time and patience. As it developed slowly, little by little, it moved Andrea a little farther along in her confidence in encountering others. Each little encounter made her a little less nervous, and a little more emboldened for the next time, the next person or situation that called to her.

Now Andrea understands that these are everyday encounters along the way of life that allow us to follow Jesus wholeheartedly. They are happening around her all the time. The only difference is whether she notices them and whether she is willing and able to respond to them—to be interrupted and to take the risk to enter this sacred space where God is at work like the Good Samaritan did in Luke 10. Knowing that God is at work in these situations long before we arrive and long after we leave relieves us of the pressure of fixing or solving anything. We are simply used by God in whatever small way in the moment, for a time, as God does the lifelong work of calling people to himself. Andrea knew and trusted that others were also being nudged into Tanya's life and loss. Each person's life is a very big puzzle. Perhaps we are only one or two small pieces.

When Nicodemus came to Jesus by night, the encounter did not last long, and there was no conclusion to the conversation. At first, Nicodemus is quite confused by what Jesus says to him. But the Scripture does not reveal if he eventually understood or if there was any impact in his life. The story is left wide open. Jesus planted a seed. Others were left to water and perhaps harvest what Jesus began.

Andrea came to realize this principle in her relatively brief encounter with Tanya. Andrea may never know what if any impact beyond kindness that her words and prayers had on Tanya's life. But if Jesus was content to plant a seed, Andrea was encouraged that she can be content with even the small encounters she has with others.

Further reflection revealed to Andrea that there was a significant and new challenge for her in these daily encounters. Andrea described that It was easy for her to be involved in very concrete ways. It was easy to volunteer fixed amounts of time, bring meals, give money to people in need because in all these actions Andrea was in control. Andrea has a counseling degree, and It was easy for her to work with friends and mothers and kids she knew, or people that sought her out. It was much harder for Andrea to enter where she was not in control and did not know what the outcome would be. She was less versed and much less comfortable in approaching a stranger. Following Jesus meant being spontaneous, taking risks, and responding to the call, the nudge, and acting on her faith without knowing where it would lead or how long it would continue. In this case with Tanya, Andrea finally decided there was no time like the present to take the risk and trust the Lord with the outcome.

Day by day, encounter by encounter Andrea is learning to pay attention, to listen, and to answer the call when it comes. This is what it means to follow Jesus. Following Jesus means paying attention to others around us. It requires that we allow our plans and our tightly held schedules to be interrupted. It means we are not in control and we might be if a person experiences our reaching out as intrusion. But we offer ourselves, on a train platform or in a public restroom, just in case God is calling us to be a part of what He is doing in another person's life. Following Jesus means taking risks and leaving the outcome up to God. After all, it is God's mission, and we simply offer ourselves in service to that mission no matter how large a small a part we might play. Jesus risked everything for the world. Certainly, we can risk a little.

For God so loved the world that He gave His only Son.
John 3:16

Second Chances

Jessica was on the church patio after worship to take sign-ups for the fall women's retreat. She was a steady volunteer and always ready to serve wherever needed to encourage and facilitate participation in the life of the ministry and mission of her church. Jessica was actively involved in both. She had been part of two different mission teams to Africa. She went to Malawi in 2016 and had recently returned in June of 2017 from Ecuador. Jessica was also a regular contributor to the discipleship ministry of the church. She belonged to a small group, served on the Discipleship Committee, and in the spring of 2016, she participated in *Groundings.* This experience even changed the way Jessica saw her volunteering on the patio.

Several women came to the sign-up table on the patio after worship, and Jessica handed out retreat flyers and answered their questions. One of the women who came to the table was new. At leas

Jessica had never seen her before. Jessica launched into the standard retreat promotional talk. She said hello. She handed the woman a flyer and said, "It's going to be great. You should go." The woman responded that she had never been to a women's retreat before, then added, "I grew up Catholic."

Jessica, attempting to make her feel more comfortable, replied, "I grew up Catholic, too. And I have never been on a retreat either. But I have been doing all sorts of things I have never done before. I am going on this retreat."

The woman looked surprised, and said, "Really?"

Jessica could tell she was very unsure about attending such an event. The woman explained that she did not know anything about this kind of event or Bible verses—or much about the Bible at all. Now the standard promotional talk was inadequate. Trying to further encourage the woman Jessica told her that she was just beginning to learn more about the Bible herself. The woman looked surprised but not convinced. She said she would think about it as she walked away head down reading the flyer Jessica had given to her.

As soon as she was walking away Jessica thought to herself, *that was a potential Groundings experience. And, I missed it. I blew it. I should have asked her more questions and found out more about her.* Jessica was disappointed in herself. She had not even asked the woman her name. She knew that God can use these simple encounters for significant kingdom work. She tried to pay attention and notice when these

opportunities came, but she was still learning. She had missed this one, or so she thought.

The next day Jessica was on her way to Costco to get gas and get her car washed. On her way to Costco, for some reason, the woman from the patio after worship came to her mind again. She was still wishing she had taken more time to talk with her. After her car was filled with gas and washed, Jessica decided to grab lunch at Costco. *After all*, she thought, *you can't beat the prices. A huge slice of pizza is $1.99 and a soft drink is $0.59. A hotdog and drink combo is $1.50. If you want to go more healthy, you can get a Caesar salad for $3.99.*[4]

For Jessica, like most people, the lunch idea was convenient and not a regular meal plan. But, lo and behold, the Spirit of God is even active in the Costco food court. As Jessica walked back to find a table to enjoy her pizza, she was completely surprised to see the woman from the church patio on Sunday. Though Jessica failed to ask her name and felt like she missed an opportunity to encounter the woman more significantly, Jessica could not believe she saw the same woman sitting there at Costco. This certainly was no coincidence. The Lord was giving Jessica a second chance—a make-up *Groundings* experience. But how to go about it?

The woman was occupied with an e-reader, and Jessica did not want to interrupt her. Jessica decided to sit across from the table where the woman was sitting and maybe Jessica would get her attention and have the chance to get to know her better and encourage her more about attending the women's retreat. Jessica would not miss this *Groundings* experience a second time. This time Jessica was paying closer attention and waiting for the right time to engage this woman. She was also praying, "Lord, thank you for this second chance. Help me to not miss it. I am willing. Use me." Finally, the woman looked up from her reader and looked right at Jessica. There was no missing this opportunity. Jessica immediately said, "Hey, didn't we talk on the patio at church yesterday?"

The woman replied, "Yes we did."

Jessica continued, "I can't believe it. In the car on the way here, I was actually thinking about you. I did not get your name yesterday."

The woman looked surprised and pleased at the same time and said, "My name is Carol. Carol Simpson."

Jessica was so excited and reciprocated with, "My name is Jessica. Jessica Patterson. I am so glad to see you again."

The woman invited Jessica to come and sit with her, and they talked for a long time. Jessica was stunned at how open Carol was about her life. It was more confirmation that this was no happenstance encounter. The Spirit of God had an appointment for Jessica with this woman and was not about to let her miss it.

Carol told Jessica that she was a regular beach walker at Dana Point. Jessica was amazed when Carol went on and shared that she used to walk with her husband but that he had died just a few months ago.

questions for small group processing to assist these devoted followers of Christ to understand how the particular truths would unpack in their context and culture. This challenge was no small task. But, I believe I had been given this opportunity in order to ensure that what I eventually would teach here in Southern California would, indeed, be stripped of cultural and contextual biases as much as possible. I would come to realize much later that the Spirit of God was not primarily interested in my curriculum being stripped of biases. My heart and mind needed to be stripped and transformed (See Introduction, pages 9-14). The Lord would use these Malawian brothers and sisters to help me do this.

Though Malawi does have its own language, Chichewa, and multiple dialects too, most of the people I would be working with spoke English. Occasionally one of the local leaders would stop me and translate something in Chichewa that they felt was a little challenging for the audience in English. I asked them to do this as often as they needed. This reality forced me to slow down and to narrow the focus of what I was teaching. It is always humbling when you travel to foreign countries and people there speak multiple languages, including English. And they are apologizing for their poor English.

What I experienced in Malawi was humbling and inspiring all at once. It completely transformed my understanding of the power of God's Word to transcend time and space. I will try to recreate the experience of teaching just two of the principles of *Groundings* and I believe they will suffice to demonstrate this.

Jesus-like hospitality in Malawi is on a scale few in the United States ever will experience or be called on to extend. For Southern California believers, hospitality is primarily about inviting someone into your home for a meal or, perhaps for an overnight stay of a day or two. We are especially attuned to this kind of hospitality on holidays. Think Christmas and Thanksgiving. Hospitality means providing lots of food and space to enjoy each other's company. Decisions like, what food to serve, what dinnerware to use, and how to seat all the guests comfortably take up much of our hospitality energy.

Malawi is a world away.

There are almost one million cases of AIDS in Malawi in the population of seventeen million. Even more tragic is the more than half a million children between the ages of one and seventeen that have been orphaned by AIDS.[5] Most of the people that I was given the blessed privilege of teaching had opened their homes to children who have been orphaned by AIDS. These devout Christian couples may have two or three children of their own and then one of their relatives die, they become the parents of three more children. Their homes have been opened not for a meal or a weekend, but for many years. The decisions that come with this kind of hospitality is not what kind of food to serve, but how to acquire and pay for food to feed additional children. And, this hospitality goes beyond food. In Malawi, education is not free. These families also have to find ways to support these children in their education. In addition to finances, marriages are strained as the children of another family increase the financial and emotional weight of life on a daily basis. And often more than one relative has children that need assistance. If the choice is between whose children to take in, how does a Christian couple following Christ decide?

Hospitality for Malawians requires radical life transformation not an occasional adjustment to routine. My thinking about hospitality was radically challenged. Time after time when I asked them how they were able to do what they were doing—open their homes and lives to orphaned children—their response was always the same. They believe they have been blessed to be a blessing and that they must follow the example of Scripture in the Old and New Testaments that reveal a God who always finds room for the orphan and stranger. Jesus was a man of sorrows acquainted with grief and told His followers to expect the same.

And noticing God at work in the world also takes on elevated significance in Malawi. Malawi is one of the most underdeveloped countries in Africa and is ranked among the poorest countries in the world. Seventy-five percent of Malawi is Christian with the rich history of Presbyterian and Anglican churches being established in the late 1800's resulting from the work of Dr. David Livingston. The statistics and demographics of Malawi require a closer look to see how God is at work in the midst of the poverty and disease. It would be easy to think that God was somehow absent and miss God at work in this little country. But the evidence of God at work is overwhelming.

I have served churches in six different states in the United States. In every one of them when a discipleship course has been offered, or just about any adult class for that matter, the attendance at the beginning is good. But over the weeks the attendance goes down. The longer the class goes on, the smaller the attendance at the end. People most often attribute this decline in attendance to busy and erratic schedules. Of course, the content and quality of the course might also contribute to this decline. However, in Malawi, it is not so. My host explained to me that people would be coming from all over the country for this discipleship training. She explained that some would come by bus or by bicycle. Louise Laubscher is an amazing woman who has worked in Malawi for almost forty years herself drove a van around for a couple of hours before the classes would start, picking up people all over the area surrounding the site where the course was being taught. She explained to me that some people would arrive late because they would be walking to the training, and it might take them a day or two to arrive. In Malawi when I taught discipleship, every day *more* people arrived. The first day over twenty eager students showed up. The second day over thirty sat ready to learn when the morning session began. The third day forty-five people were facing me with anticipation. By the final day, more than fifty people attended the training. And, after traveling for hours or even days, the majority of these people were camping in tents for the duration of the training.

These were people who had jobs or needed jobs. They were people who had children or grandchildren and almost all of them had taken in other children orphaned by AIDS. Many of them suffered from a variety of illnesses themselves and all of them were struggling with having enough resources to feed, clothe, and educate their children. These were people whose lives and schedules were very complicated but somehow, they found the wherewithal to come to this training and learn from the stories of Jesus what it meant to follow Jesus. Story after story they told about their lives evidenced God at work in the midst of the poverty and disease. Story after story demonstrated their trust in the God who was at work in and through them. They never doubted it for a minute.

And these people sang and danced like nothing I have ever seen before. The joy of the Lord was their strength. Without instruments and without screens they sang and danced songs of praise to the Lord. My congregation, several times the size of this group with all of the technical and instrumental support money can buy, cannot hold a candle to their singing.

After teaching...no, *learning*...in Malawi, I was able to see the heart of the narratives of Jesus' teaching because being in Malawi stripped me of the cultural trappings and biases that so often accompany our application of the scripture. Discipleship and following Jesus into the world has to work in places where there are no Starbucks, or easy access to grocery stores, and restaurants and train stations. Being the living Christ to the world, continuing the work of Jesus has to work where disease and famine and poverty are everyday realities.

Hospitality is so much more than opening up a certain space for a limited time to others. Jesus-like hospitality is allowing your life and plans to be interrupted and radically changed for the sake of living out the love of God for the world. Proclaiming the kingdom is more than sharing the love of Jesus with friends and neighbors. It means walking or riding for days and sleeping in tents so that you can learn more about the Good News in order to share it confidently with others. Knowing your neighbor for Malawians goes way beyond helping someone by the side of the road for a day or two. It may mean helping the child of a relative for a lifetime. And, knowing the mission of God for the people of Malawi is not a theological discussion. It is a ministry that brings the hope of being born again and having eternal life to people who are struggling with life and death issues every day. God truly is at work in every square inch of the universe.

He is the atoning sacrifice for our sins,
and not only for ours but also for the
sins of the whole world.

1 John 2:2

Heart to Heart

The *Groundings* experience had taught Newt and Carol about third spaces. Carol had experienced *Groundings* a year earlier. Now Newt was in a *Groundings* group for the summer. Both of them had learned that any place any time can become a space where God is at work, and He may invite them to participate in that work. It is called a third space because it is not the space you immediately consider it to be. Nor is it the space another person thinks it is. Starbucks is not simply a coffee place or a place to work on your laptop. A person having coffee and a person on their laptop may encounter one another in a way that the space—Starbucks—becomes a space that God does kingdom work in and through the coffee drinker and the laptop worker. After years of going to the same coffee shop week after week, since beginning the *Groundings* experience Newt had begun two different conversations about spiritual things with two different people at the places he went for coffee. He had never started these kinds of conversations before. Newt was noticing God at work. And, Newt was offering himself to be part of that work. Newt spoke with great enthusiasm about these new encounters.

On a more somber occasion, Newt and Carol were together eating lunch at a restaurant. They had spent the morning at the hospital with their son and daughter-in-law and grandson, Joey. It was a monumental day. Joey was seven years old and was having open heart surgery on this day. Once Joey was taken into surgery, Newt and Carol were told to go get some lunch. Newt's son said he would call them when Joey was out of surgery. The young boy would be in recovery quite a while so they would have plenty of time to get back to the hospital when needed. Though hesitant to leave, Newt and Carol understood that they needed to eat, and they knew the time would pass more quickly this way. At a nearby restaurant, they found a booth to quietly eat their lunch. The mood was somber and serious, of course. Neither of them had much left to say.

Shortly after they were seated in the restaurant a young man had come in for lunch and had been seated in the booth right behind them. Suddenly the young man got up from his booth and came over to theirs. Newt thought he looked to be about forty-five or fifty years old. As he approached their table both Carol and Newt were a little unsettled by it. But as he approached, the young man began the conversation.

"Excuse me. I am not sure what your story is but I believe the Lord wants me to talk to you," he said with obvious kindness and a very intense look on his face. Newt and Carol looked at each other with mutual surprise and delight in their eyes. Previously, they would have thought this behavior strange and been uncomfortable with this kind of approach. But, now that they had participated in *Groundings,* they were not as surprised by this. They both were learning to pay attention to God at work in the world, and they both immediately recognized that this moment must be one of those moments.

"Well," still a bit surprised Carol began, "our grandson Joey, who is seven years old, is having open heart surgery right now. We spent the morning with his family at the hospital and now we are having lunch and waiting for a phone call from his father to let us know he is out of surgery and how the surgery went."

"This is incredible! God is incredible! Now I know for sure that I was supposed to talk to you," replied the younger man with clear amazement in his voice. "I have a story, too, and I think I am supposed to tell you my story and pray with you," his voice now filled with excitement and compassion. "You're not going to believe this. But, fifteen years ago, my son had open heart surgery. He was seven years old," the man explained with wonder in his eyes. It was true. Newt and Carol could hardly believe what they were hearing. They looked at each other totally in awe. They were overcome with emotion and their eyes were welling up with tears. The young man continued. He briefly told the story of his own son's battle for his life due to heart problems. But with hope and praise in his voice, he also described his son's miraculous recovery from open heart surgery. Then he asked, "Can I pray for you and your grandson?"

"Of course!" Newt and Carol replied in unison. This was a sacred moment, and they knew God was in it.

The young man invited them to stand up. Oh boy! Newt and Carol were not accustomed to praying in public. And especially not to standing up and praying in public. But given the wonder and amazement of this moment and these circumstances, how could they refuse? God was definitely at work here. It was just the reverse of what Newt was expecting. Instead of Newt and Carol being attentive to how they might enter into what God was doing in another person's life, here was someone who was entering into what God was doing in their own lives. When they were the ones who needed the presence and power of the living Christ, someone answered the nudge of the Spirit of God and came to them.

They stood. They held hands and this young man prayed a beautiful and compassion-filled prayer for them and for Joey and his parents. When they were done praying the man said something that Newt would never forget. He told them that God can do miracles in an instant but that healing often takes a long time. They needed to hear this. They had not yet received the phone call saying Joey was out of surgery and that it went well and that he was in recovery. They needed to know that no matter what their son said when he called, that God can do miracles, but also that healing can take a long time. The young man went back to his booth to finish his lunch. Newt and Carol sat back down but could not eat another bite. They were in awe of what had just happened.

Both Newt and Carol were developing a sense of public places being third spaces where God was at work and where God might want to use them to help with that work. And now, they had just experienced another person doing the same thing. But this time Newt and Carol were the ones God wanted to do the work in and this young man was the one God wanted to use to help do that work. What had just happened? Reverse *Groundings* had just happened. This young man was attentive to what God was up to in that restaurant. He sensed the Spirit of God prompting him. He took a risk. He made himself available. He became the face and voice of the Spirit of God reassuring Newt and Carol that God was with them and was the Great Physician, ultimately in charge of Joey's well-being.

Indeed, when we become open to God at work in the world in every place and when we listen and pay attention to what is going on around us, not only are we able to minister to others by joining in with what God is doing, others are able to minister to us in the very same way.

In the story of the woman at the well, the disciples perceived themselves as out and about with Jesus. They had been commissioned to follow Him. They were following Him into the world and presumably learning to do the work that Jesus was doing. And yet, the disciples go into the village for lunch and return with only lunch. There is no evidence of any interaction with the people from the place (third space?) where they went to buy lunch. And they brought no one back with them. They had been traveling and learning from Jesus, and Jesus was always interacting with the people He encountered wherever He went. Granted, this was Samaria, and Jews did not socialize with Samaritans. But while Jews did not socialize with Samaritans, sinners, or tax collectors, or lepers, Jesus did. And they had been observing Jesus doing this day after day.

Now they observe Him interacting, not only with a Samaritan but a woman. They are perplexed and questioned Jesus' behavior. And, astounding as it may seem, the woman now became the disciples' teacher. After a significant personal and theological conversation with Jesus at the well, the woman who came for much-needed water, dropped her water jars and ran back to the village. She did not take time out to go to evangelism training or Bible school. The account says she immediately left her water jars and ran back to the village and burst into her neighborhood and home. She invited everyone she encountered to come and hear this man who had told her everything about herself. She began her confession right away when she said to them, "Could this be the Messiah?"

The text says that a crowd followed her back to the well. This Samaritan woman had only been with Jesus for a very short time and yet she was bringing others to hear Him. She was an evangelist. The disciples had been following Jesus for months and had been having conversations with Him and sitting at his feet for a long time. Yet, when they went into the village they brought no one back to hear Him. The woman noticed God at work at this well, and she participated in that work. This Samaritan woman was teaching the disciples what it meant to notice God and work and to make oneself available to be part of it. The woman responded personally. She was pondering, *Could this be the Messiah?* She was inviting others then and continues to invite us now, to come and ponder the same question. "Come and see [Jesus] for yourself!"

The well that provides a resting place for Jesus and the disciples and life-giving water for the village is a third space where God is at work proclaiming the Good News of the Gospel. In this space, Jesus is inviting men and women, Jews and Samaritans, and anyone else willing to pay attention to be reconciled and to join Him in reconciling the world to himself. It was an invitation to discipleship. It was an invitation to see the whole world as one enormous third space. It was an invitation to be amazed and in awe of God's work in and all around us every moment of every day.

The invitation stands. The work goes both ways. The work is in us, and the work is through us. But the work is also through others, to us. Newt and Carol had this reverse *Groundings* experience that day while eating lunch. Their attentiveness to noticing God at work was expanded significantly that day. They will never see a restaurant the same way. Focused and fearful about the well-being of their grandson Joey, they were taught by a stranger, a young man also eating lunch, that God was at work the whole time.

God was at work in the operating room. God was at work in the restaurant. And, God had been at work for years preparing this time when one young man whose son had experienced open heart surgery was noticing God at work in a restaurant. Years of God at work in his life now came to bear as this young man would participate in the lives of two others whose grandson was now having open heart surgery and were also learning to notice God at work.

Oh, the wonder of the ways of God. With the Psalmist we proclaim, "How high are your ways! Who can know them?" Paul quotes from that Psalm in Romans 11:33-36.

Oh, the depth of the riches of the wisdom and knowledge of God!
How unsearchable His judgments,
and his paths beyond tracing out!
"Who has known the mind of the Lord?
Or who has been his counselor?"
"Who has ever given to God,
that God should repay them?"
For from Him and through Him and
for Him are all things.
To him be the glory forever! Amen.
Romans 11:33-36

Rachel the Recycler

Have you ever learned a new word and then noticed people using it all the time? Or been introduced to a new song, and then it seems you hear it everywhere you go? Why does this happen? Are people using the word more in conversation or print? Are radio stations playing the song more, or the internet streaming the song more often, or are people posting it on Facebook more than before? No. You are hearing the word or the song more because now you know about it and are noticing it. God wants us to know enough about His kingdom and the work of His Kingdom to be able to notice it. If we say that we want to follow Christ, then we must follow Him into the world and pay attention to where Christ is working both in our own lives and in the lives of those all around us. God is always at work. God in Christ is building the Kingdom of Heaven right here on earth one person at a time, brick by brick. But we are all connected in the Kingdom God is building. At any moment in time, God wants to use me in the building of another person's life. And at other moments God can use what He is doing in another person's life to build into my life. We often become so focused on our private little kingdom building at work or at home that we have no time or attention to give to noticing what God is up to in building His kingdom that will last forever. Even when we take the time, God's work is so dynamic and fluid, paying attention and noticing it takes concentrated effort.

Before Sheryl experienced *Groundings,* she had occasionally noticed a woman walking down the street outside her office window. When Sheryl took the time to observe more closely, she saw the woman almost every day and watched her picking through the neighbor's recycling bins. Sheryl works at a large Presbyterian Church. It is an imposing structure with a huge sign facing the street where this woman was picking. The woman certainly knew this was a church. On one occasion when Sheryl saw her picking she went out to talk to her. The woman was wearing earbuds and listening to music as she collected. She did not notice Sheryl until she was right beside her. It was a bit awkward, and she did not take the earbuds out. Still, Sheryl asked her what her name was. The woman responded, Sheryl said, "But of course, I promptly forgot her name and went back to work." Really listening and then remembering is always a challenge. The intense concentration on listening in the *Groundings* experience has made Sheryl aware of the importance of listening and has helped her to grow in her ability to listen.

In Matthew 26:44 Jesus said, "Simon, look at this woman." It was not that Simon had not been looking at her. He had seen her and was disgusted. He had whispered to the other men, "If He [Jesus] was a prophet He would know what kind of woman this was," meaning, Jesus would not let her touch Him. Jesus told Simon to look again and to see her differently. Now, Jesus was telling Sheryl the same thing—to look again and to see this woman differently.

A couple of weeks later, Sheryl saw the woman again. This time because she saw her differently, Sheryl knew that God was calling her to interrupt her personal schedule. After all, she worked in a church, and she was doing God's work. But this, too, was God's work. God was calling Sheryl to encounter this can-collecting woman again and, this time, to see her with the eyes of Jesus.

This time Sheryl planned ahead and put some cans from the office in a bag. The next time she saw the woman, Sheryl allowed herself to be interrupted. She took the bag of cans out to the woman. This time the woman took the earbuds out of her ears, and Sheryl began a conversation with her, first about recycling, but the conversation went on from there.

The encounter was surprisingly comfortable this time. She told Sheryl her name was Rachel and since it started with 'R', now Sheryl would never forget "Rachel the recycler." This time Rachel also asked if the woman would tell her story—which she did. Sheryl listened. Rachel had a son. She collected cans to help pay their bills. It was a fascinating story, and it was clear that God was already at work in Rachel's life. Through the *Groundings* experience, Sheryl knew that she was not the first one on the scene. God had been there before. God had now invited Sheryl to come alongside and listen and observe and learn. So often when we think about sharing the Good News with others, we think about talking to them and telling them what we know that they need to hear. When we understand that God is already at work in the lives of others long before we ever show up, we listen first. We do not have to know exactly what to say. We can simply ask questions and listen.

After this encounter, Sheryl made a point to bring cans to the office to give to Rachel as an expression of kindness—an expression of God's care for Rachel through her. Sheryl did not have to say it, but Sheryl represented God and what she was doing was in God's name. What this woman told Sheryl later confirmed that the woman understood that Sheryl's kindness was from the Lord.

So often when we encounter people we think that we are starting from scratch. We think we have the whole weight of the person's eternity in our hands and on our shoulders. We forget that God is the Hound of Heaven[6] who relentlessly pursues those He calls to himself. Over time, listening to Rachel the recycler, Sheryl learned that part of Rachel's story actually began at the same church where Sheryl worked. Years before Sheryl began working at the church, God was calling to Rachel through the church. Rachel had attended preschool at the church when she was a child. God had begun His work many years before Sheryl showed up.

Rachel told Sheryl that she had also attended another church later in life with a pastor that Sheryl knew. Again, it was clear, God had been working in this woman's life before Sheryl ever showed up. God beat Sheryl to Rachel. God was at work in Sheryl's life through Rachel, too. As Sheryl took the time to notice God at work and learned to be quiet long enough to hear, she began to see what God was up to. Sheryl does not know the full effect of her encounter with Rachel, but since Sheryl did not begin the story, she knew that she did not have to finish it either. Sheryl was simply one piece of a large puzzle God was putting together in the story being written to communicate His compelling love for Rachel.

Eventually, Rachel stopped walking and picking down the street past the church. It was a long time before Sheryl saw her again. But one day she saw her walking in another part of town. Sheryl took the time to stop and talk to her again. Rachel had moved and had found a different area to walk and pick. God was still working in Rachel's life. And God was still working in Sheryl's life, too. Perhaps the bulk of the work God was doing in this case, was in Sheryl's life. The Lord was actually using Rachel to teach Sheryl more about how God works.

Sheryl never saw her again. But she learned so much from the encounter with Rachel. Another woman took up collecting on the street past the church. This time Sheryl did not wait. She grabbed some cans and went out to talk with this new woman. This woman spoke Spanish. In the way only God can provide, at the same time, another church employee who spoke Spanish was coming out of the building. Sheryl called him over and with his help interpreting, she was able to learn this woman's name and give her the cans. The Spanish-speaking employee also invited this woman to the Spanish language worship service. Sheryl does not know if she ever came. It does not matter; what matters is how God teaches us to pay attention. He teaches us to listen. He teaches us to allow our routines to be interrupted. He shows us that when we pay attention—notice what is going on around us—God can use every encounter as a piece of the puzzle of His grand story. We begin to look at people differently. We may be interrupted a lot, but God is at work in us and through us, and there is no turning back.

The story of the woman at the well powerfully demonstrates this kingdom work and how God in Christ goes about it. Jesus began the conversation right where the woman was—at the well gathering water. Jesus asked her for something she could give Him as a bridge to offer her something that only He could give her. She was surprised. Jesus, a man and obviously a Jew, was breaking all sorts of cultural norms to engage with her. She revealed a large part of the reason she was an outcast, hardened by years of derision and ostracism and shame, and the reason she was at the well when no one else was—she had had several husbands and currently was living with a man who was not her husband. Jesus' tone of voice must have been empathetic and compassionate because she remained and continued to talk to Him and to listen. The woman at the well was so taken with what she Jesus was saying, that eventually, leaving her water jug behind, she turned and ran to the village to get others to come and hear Jesus.

However, before she left, the disciples returned from the town where they had gone to get food. The disciples had not yet learned what Sheryl has learned. They did not know that God in Christ was at work in others—people they disdained and despised. They did not know that listening to other people's stories was a means of telling the Good News. So the disciples were perplexed and dismayed that Jesus was talking to a Samaritan woman. They were looking right at her and did not see her. They did not see the woman the way Jesus saw her. But perhaps the most astounding part of this woman's story was how God used it. Broken and outcast, she is the one who immediately began to evangelize. The disciples who had been following Jesus for some time went into town for lunch and brought no one back with them to hear and learn from Jesus. The despised and outcast Samaritan woman ran back to town and brought a crowd, family, neighbors, and strangers—everyone she met—to come and hear this man, Jesus. No one that day believed Jesus because of the disciple's testimonies. Many believe that day because of the woman's testimony (John 4:39).

God is at work everywhere even in the least likely places and in the least likely people. God is working in and through them to tell the Good News of the

Gospel that in Christ Jesus, God is reconciling the world to himself. Rachel taught Sheryl this powerful lesson. The Samaritan woman at the well taught the disciples. Any space can be a place where the Lord does his reconciling work. Any person can be a person God uses to tell and to hear the Good news. The difference is whether or not we are paying attention and taking the time to stop and see what God is doing and then determining if we are supposed to be part of that work.

The Lord is not slow in keeping his promise,
as some understand slowness. Instead He
is patient with you, not wanting anyone to
perish, but everyone to come to repentance.
2 Peter 3:9

Semper Fi

Hector first met JW when Hector was placed in a new department as a military-civilian subcontractor in 2010. JW had served in the United States Marines for twenty years. Hector had served thirty years before being honorably discharged. In one way or another, they had both worked for the same organization for most of their adult lives. But as they worked in the office cubicles next to each other over the next eighteen months, they realized they had a lot more in common than being former Marines now working as civilian contractors for companies providing services to the United State Marines.

Hector and JW were both BMW motorcycle riders, 1980's music fans, and trivia buffs. Further enhancing their connection they were both classic movie fanatics. For Hector and JW "classics" meant cult classics, all James Bond flicks, and the Star Wars series. Now, they were both what is known in the military-civilian contract business as niche specialists in their jobs. They respected each other professionally. Perhaps the greatest connection was that they appreciated each other's humor when very few others did. This connection and cheerfulness was a great asset in the mundane world of military-civilian subcontracting.

In mid-2011, Hector's work took him to another location on base. But he remained in contact with JW and others that worked with him. Through the work grapevine, Hector found out that JW had been diagnosed with Leukemia and consequently had been absent from work a lot. Coworkers said that he seemed to be doing "OK." By the end of 2013, Hector was back working in the cubicle next to JW, who had survived his bout with Leukemia and seemed to be back to work as usual. Their friendship picked right back up where it had left off, cemented by the establishment of a shared pot of coffee each work day. Hector did not remember asking JW about how he was doing. Thinking back on it now, he was embarrassed that fear of being intrusive or fear of rejection, or just plain lack of concern must have prevented him from asking. He now knows better.

In the fall of 2014, Hector participated in his first *Groundings* experience. When *Groundings* kicked off, Hector was meeting JW three days a week at lunch-time to run two miles together. Because of *Groundings,* Hector had already felt prompted to open a discussion with JW regarding spiritual matters, but had never gotten the conversation off the ground. Following the first *Groundings* assignment, Hector had a renewed resolve to open the discussion with

JW. At the same time, Hector's resolve was renewed, JW's follow-up appointment schedule related to his Leukemia ramped up, and JW had to back out of their lunchtime running. Hector was concerned about JW and disappointed in himself for not having initiated a conversation with him of a spiritual nature earlier. However, they remained casual friends and professional associates.

In the fall of 2016, Hector participated in his second *Groundings* experience. He was still working with JW, but the office space had been rearranged. Though on the same floor, Hector was now in a different area so they were no longer sharing a pot of coffee. JW had room for a coffee pot on a credenza directly behind him, and Hector had switched to drinking decaf and was purchasing his morning coffee from the vendor across the street. These details that would previously have eluded Hector now were noticed as they related to wondering about what God was doing in the lives of other people, particularly, JW's life at this time. Now prompted by the *Groundings* assignment after the second session, Hector felt compelled to step out of his comfort zone and ask JW how he was doing and to find a way to ask him about his personal faith journey and what he believed about God.

Hector was on high alert, paying close attention for the right opportunity to have this conversation with JW. Much to Hector's frustration almost two weeks passed seemingly without that opportunity. It was now the afternoon before *Groundings* Session three that evening when Hector was supposed to report on his assignment from session two, and

Hector still had not talked to JW. Hector was feeling frustrated and guilty. *Why was this so hard?*

Hector worked a little late that day. He had packed a light dinner and was planning on eating it at his desk before heading to *Groundings*. Just then, Hector saw JW across the room walking in the direction of his cubicle. Perhaps JW was working late as well. Hector was not absolutely sure that this was the opportune moment, but clearly, time was running out. So Hector decided to take the chance. He picked up his packed dinner and went to the area where JW was now working. There was JW working at his desk. He was working late, too. Hector cleared a spot on JW's credenza and asked if he minded if Hector ate his dinner there. JW was fine with it. JW motioned for Hector to pull over a chair and sit down.

It seemed to Hector that it was now or never. As Hector had learned from the stories about Jesus encountering others, Hector began the conversation with exactly where Hector knew JW was—in recovery from his bout with leukemia. The wording was probably very awkward, but the intention was pure. Hector wanted to see what JW was thinking about faith and God in light of his battle with this disease. Hector asked him how he was doing, and after listening awhile followed up with a deeper question. Hector asked JW if his bout with Leukemia had impacted his faith or what he believed about God.

JW acknowledged that Leukemia was a totally "real" experience. JW said that facing the disease eliminated the esoteric and totally theoretical ideas about faith and God and boiled it down to brass tacks.

Hector thought he knew what JW was talking about, but before Hector had a chance to ask him to explain, JW began talking about his spiritual experiences going all the way back into his childhood.

JW told Hector that his parents had sent him to a private religious school. JW began talking about experiences from his middle school days at this school. And though many of the details and circumstances were missing, JW was vividly describing how he felt at the time and how what he felt had influenced his views about faith and God. JW remembered some of his teachers and the religious nature of their instruction. But it was other members of the staff of that school that had the most impact on spiritually shaping JW. As JW put it, it was the "less spiritually oriented" staff at the school that made the greatest impact on him when it came to living his faith day to day. JW explained that he was much more impressed by two guys that worked in the school cafeteria than the spiritual figure heads that were his religion teachers. Listening to JW's story, it was now Hector who was learning about how God works in and through people. Clearly, faith was not foreign to JW. Hector was not the first to talk with him about faith and the presence of God. The Spirit of God had been working in JW through others for a very long time.

JW described his success at spitting back to his religion teachers what they wanted to hear—the right answers. He also revealed to Hector that he had taken top honors in his religion classes three years in a row. But it was the way the cafeteria workers served and talked to and listened to JW and the students that left the greatest impression on JW. These employees were real to JW. The emotions of his current fight against Leukemia brought back memories of his days in religion classes that did not seem real while the conversation in the cafeteria with cafeteria employees felt very real. Now much more engaged with JW's story, Hector felt compelled to ask him if these early experiences of his religious teachers being less real to him than cafeteria workers had resulted in a distancing of himself from the spiritual and God. JW immediately protested that he "wouldn't say that—wouldn't say that at all!" Somehow what JW learned in his head in class was refined and made more real by what he learned in the cafeteria in his heart.

Hector and JW talked for a good forty-five minutes when Hector realized that he had to leave to make it to *Groundings* on time. Hector thought about how ironic this was. He had procrastinated in talking to JW so long that he now had to cut this conversation with him short in order to get to the class on time. The *Groundings* experience that had given him the assignment was now encroaching on his assignment! But, Hector had made significant progress in following Christ into the world—the world of his own office. And Hector was eager to get to *Groundings* and share his experience with others in his small group. He was definitely noticing God at work in other people's lives and learning to take the time to be a good neighbor in every day places like the office. This time he would not go to *Groundings* empty-handed.

This experience forced Hector to re-examine the whole idea of third spaces and who his "neighbors" might be. He had been looking in other places to see how God might be at work in and around him. But he had not included the seemingly nonspiritual place where he worked. And though JW was not left to die by the side of the road, like the victim in the story of the Good Samaritan in Luke 10, JW was a victim of Leukemia and sitting by his desk waiting for someone to come alongside and listen and help him process what he had experienced. Just as the Good Samaritan came alongside the man left for dead, Hector came alongside JW still recovering from a bout with Leukemia.

The workplace is a little tricky. For a variety of reasons, some work environments are more or less conducive to these kinds of conversations of significance. Some companies with more litigious mindset actually prohibit such conversations in the workplace. But the majority of work environments have some freedom of time or where the necessary tasks are amenable to brief conversations. In most work environments, personal meal and break time certainly are open to third-space conversations.

This experience was totally world-tilting for Hector. He continues to try to come to grips with this reality. Hector knows now that any space can be a third space. Hector knows that every space is open to God at work in and through people in order to accomplish God's mission of reconciling the world to himself in Christ. The encounter has been six years in the making, and now it has been nine months since this interrupted *Groundings* conversation between Hector and JW, and Hector's waiting and watching for another opportunity to pick up where they left off. If Hector does not, you can be sure that by the grace of God and the presence of the Spirit of God, someone else will. In *The Gospel Medicine,* Barbara Brown Taylor says it like this in talking about the presence of Christ in the world after He ascended to the Father in the world she says,

"It was almost as if He had not ascended but exploded, so that all the holiness that was once concentrated in Him alone flew everywhere, flew far and wide so that the seeds of heaven were sown in all the fields of the earth." [7]

Who can hide in secret places
so that I cannot see them?"
declares the LORD.
"Do not I fill heaven and earth?"
declares the LORD.
Jeremiah. 23:24

Email Opportunity

Craig received an email from Raj. The email seemed to come completely out of the blue. Craig remembered a guy named Raj from his college days. An unusual name. Hard to forget. If Craig remembered correctly, Raj was a freshman when Craig was a senior in college. But Craig had not seen or had any contact with Raj since Craig left college in 1978. Thirty-nine years had passed. As a freshman and a senior, they were on different college schedules. And though they were both on the football team and pledged the same fraternity, they were not close friends.

When the email first showed up in Craig's inbox, he thought it was a scam. Craig, like most of us, was constantly dealing with strange emails filling his inbox from who knows where. He was suspicious about this particular email. Even if it really was from Raj, his college fraternity and football acquaintance, why was he getting it now, thirty-nine years later? And if it was Raj from college, Craig wondered how Raj got his email. Craig suspected the email was fishing for something.

Nothing was attached, so there seemed no risk in opening it so Craig clicked on the email to read it. Craig quickly realized that the email was a personal one and likely from his college friend. Raj wrote about some hard times, admitting that he had made some bad decisions and that those decisions were largely responsible for his current bad situation. Among the problems Raj described, were the fact that he was struggling to pay his rent and medical bills. He told Craig that he didn't have any friends from college. He said that he remembered Craig being a nice guy and so he was reaching out to him. This was the explanation Raj gave for contacting Craig after thirty-nine years. In that first email, Raj said all he wanted was someone to talk with.

Even though Craig had determined the email really was from his college acquaintance, he still was a bit suspicious about why Raj had decided to contact him. When Craig read that Raj was struggling to pay his bills, he immediately suspected Raj was going to ask Craig for money. But Raj did not ask for money. Not in the first email. And in Craig's surprise that Raj did not ask for money, Craig wondered if this email might be the start of a *Groundings* experience—a *Groundings* experience via email. Craig had never considered the possibility that an email could be a third space—a place where God was at work in the lives of people corresponding over the internet.

Craig reflected on the peculiarity and timing of this communication from his college acquaintance and determined there was no other way that he would get this email from Raj after not hearing from him or seeing him for almost forty years. Craig was learning to pay attention to God at work in the world. Certainly, the world of the internet is not out of God's influence. It now seemed that God's fingerprints were all over the circumstances and timing of this communication. Craig also knew that God's purposes in these kinds of encounters are not only to minister to the other person but for Craig to learn more about how to do the work of Jesus in the world—even the world of the internet. Now there was no doubt in his mind. Craig knew this was a *Groundings* experience.

The next day, Craig wrote back to Raj, saying how surprised he was to hear from him. Craig sincerely conveyed his sympathy for the difficult situation Raj found himself in. Craig empathized with Raj and told him that he, too, had made many bad decisions earlier in his life. Then Craig shared part of his faith story with Raj. He told Raj that in spite of the bad decisions, he was much different now. Craig explained to Raj that he was a Christian, that Jesus was his Savior and that his life had been radically changed through faith in Christ. Craig then took the next step in his email conversation with Raj. He opened up the spiritual conversation further with him by asking Raj if he believed in Jesus. After a little more closing email small talk, Craig signed off and pushed send. Then he waited.

Raj did not respond for more than a week. Craig thought that his comments and questions about Jesus had scared Raj away. But, about ten days later, Craig received another email from Raj. In this email, Raj responded to Craig's inquiry about Jesus. He told

Craig that he had an "on and off" relationship with Jesus. Raj expressed how happy he was that Craig had responded to his email and was communicating with him. Raj said that it really helped him deal with his situation. Then, in this second email, just as Craig had suspected he would, Raj asked Craig for money.

Craig went through the range of thoughts and feelings that we all do when we are confronted with helping someone in great need. He knew that either response held risks. If Craig agreed to send money, it could set up an ongoing expectation for financial help. Given the circumstances Raj described he was in, Craig knew that Raj's financial circumstances were way beyond Craig's ability to assist. Even if Craig helped Raj financially at that time, the relationship could be jeopardized eventually if Craig ever declined to send him more money. But Craig also knew that if he did not send any money to Raj, the communication could end abruptly and Craig's opportunity to help Raj see how God might be at work in all of these circumstances could be lost. This just-beginning *Groundings* experience could come to a screeching halt. There was no easy answer. Craig thought and prayed about it.

Craig also talked with his wife about the request and together they decided not to send Raj any money. But Craig was willing to offer his friendship and to continue the conversation about Jesus. Craig decided to trust the Lord with where the conversation went and remembered that even Jesus didn't always see the end result of his spiritual conversations. In Luke 18, Jesus responded to the question of a rich young ruler. The Bible records that the young man walked away sad. Sometimes God uses his disciples in small ways to plant a seed that someone else will be used to water, or to water a seed that someone else will tend. Craig reminded himself, it is God that is at work in each of us to will and to do his good pleasure (Philippians 2:13). In the story of Nicodemus in John 3, after all the back and forth between Jesus and Nicodemus, we are never told what happened regarding the faith of Nicodemus. The last we hear from Nicodemus in the story is in verse nine when he asked, "How can these things be?" Sounds like there was more work to be done in the life of Nicodemus.

Craig is a regular volunteer and avid supporter of a ministry in his hometown that assists families in need so he knew there were organizations out there that could help someone like Raj. After he did a little research, Craig sent another email to Raj regarding agencies where Raj lived that might be able to help him with paying bills and maybe even help him find affordable housing. Craig *was* offering financial assistance, but in a way that was more likely to help Raj in the long run. He was offering help that depended on the wisdom of someone closer to Raj's circumstances to make the right decisions about how best to help him. Often, being present and participating in what God is doing in another person's life means pointing them in the right direction, not actually solving their problem. Craig waited for Raj's response with some trepidation, fearing Raj might not respond at all or might respond hurt or angry.

Craig's fears were not realized. Truly God was in the middle of this email *Groundings* experience and orchestrating all the details. In the next email, Raj said that he understood Craig's decision not to send him money. Craig was relieved. Raj also said that he valued the friendship more than the money and Craig was grateful for this. Raj asked Craig to please continue corresponding via the emails. Craig was a little disappointed that Raj did not say anything more in the second email about starting a relationship with Jesus. But Craig allowed the Scripture to help him not be discouraged. In Corinthians Paul instructs that different people play different roles in the spreading of the good news. One plants, another waters, and the Lord alone is responsible for the end result—the harvest (1 Corinthians 3:6-7). And Craig remembered what he learned in *Groundings* about the importance of listening to the story of another person and trusting the Spirit of God to create opportunities to share God's love and grace with others or trusting that the Lord will bring someone else to continue that work.

Craig plans to continue the email conversations and friendship with Raj and will continue to pay attention to what God is doing in Raj's life. Craig will continue to listen to Raj and to the Spirit of God leading him in this email relationship. Perhaps the Lord will allow Craig to see how he is working in Raj's life and help Raj to see it, too. Perhaps someone else will pick up where Craig leaves off. One thing we know, that the Lord of the harvest is relentless in His pursuit of loving people. In Christ, God is not willing that any perish but is reconciling the world—all things—

to Himself through the blood of Christ (2 Peter 3:9; Colossians 1:20).

For God was pleased to have all his fullness dwell in Him, and through Him to reconcile to himself all things, whether things on earth or things in heaven, by making peace through his blood, shed on the cross.

Colossians 1:19-20

Who is the Host?

Mike and Jolene's son David, and daughter-in-law Linh were home for a visit. David went to see a friend and Linh asked if she could invite some friends over for dinner. The guest list included a girlfriend and two gay men who had worked with Linh previously, and a friend of theirs who Linh did not know. Mike and Jolene were not expecting to host such a diverse group but out of desire to help Linh see her friends, and to express their love for their daughter-in-law, they said, yes, of course.

The dinner would be hosted at Mike and Jolene's home, but the hospitality would be shared. Linh and her friends did all the meal planning and shopping. It was good that they did. The shopping list was very different. The variety of food was amazing! Small octopus, a strange type of shrimp, and soup with vegetables they had never heard of, barbecued marinated meat, and all kinds of unusual sauces covered the counters in Jolene and Mike's kitchen.

They were eager to just spend time with their daughter-in-law watching and learning about the preparation of these unfamiliar Vietnamese foods.

Mike and Jolene thought that these young people would want to eat by themselves. They did not anticipate or expect that they would be joining them for dinner. But that is exactly what happened. Linh and the guests wanted Mike and Jolene to eat with them. Mike and Jolene were surprised but delighted to join them. Being a student of *Groundings,* Jolene could not help but wonder, now who was doing the hosting? Could this evening and her home become a third space where perhaps Jesus himself would be the host?

The evening air was perfect so they decided to eat outside on the patio. The sky was clear and the sunset was spectacular. All this was only eclipsed by the amazing diverse company that was shared. With such a diverse and unfamiliar group of young people the potential for discomfort and prejudice was significant. But there was a stronger dynamic at work in this gathering. Jolene's attentiveness to what she had learned in *Groundings* about Jesus' way of encountering people that others dismissed or marginalized kept her mind and heart open to some bigger story that might be emerging in this space. And, the fact that the hospitality continued to move around only reinforced her sense that the Spirit of God was at work on this night.

Though the meal was hosted in their home, instead of Jolene and Mike serving their guests, their guests were the ones serving them. There were so many unusual circumstances in the evening. They all contributed to Jolene being much more attentive to what was happening and curious about what this shared meal might mean. So many new foods and flavors, the meal was a variety show for the palate! So many different people all with unique and stories also unfamiliar to Jolene and Mike. It was delicious, a real feast of food and people! Jolene and Mike were very curious about both. They started with the easier conversation—the food. Jolene asked a bunch of questions about the food and the traditions of how they were served and prepared these foods in their own families. It was an added pleasure to learn so much about these cultural distinctions directly from young people who knew them so well.

Prompted by her engagement with *Groundings,* Jolene wanted to get beyond the conversation about food and learn more about the young people, especially about their faith traditions. Jolene thanked them for sharing this rich cultural experience with their foods and for showing such extraordinary hospitality in so graciously preparing and serving food to her and Mike. She asked them if they might be willing to also share their cultural experience of faith. She asked them what kind of faith tradition were they raised in.

Linh's girlfriend and two of the young men shared that they were brought up Catholic. But much like every family's faith traditions, even these Catholic experiences varied significantly from one family to another. Some were very devout in their Catholic upbringing. Others, were only nominally associated with the Catholic Church. Linh shared that her family was not particularly religious at all but that she was most familiar with Buddhism. Jolene and Mike were thrilled. Due to caution and fear, and a desire to love and accept her, they had never quite been able to find a way to have this conversation with their daughter-in-law before. Linh was eager to add that she prayed a lot. Jolene found this very interesting and asked her further about how she prayed and what she believed about prayer. The other young man said that he was Buddhist. In reflecting on this conversation, Jolene realized that as the initiator of conversation, once again the hosting had moved. As inquirer of their stories, she had taken up hosting once again.

The family and their guests enjoyed this beautiful evening, delicious meal and personal conversation for a long time. The conversation continued as Jolene and Mike expressed more interest in the young people. They asked them what they were presently doing and what were their dreams? It was amazing to learn that all but one of these young friends of Linh's were interested in medical careers. They were hoping and planning on being nurses. Both gay men also wanted to become nurses and as they talked about nursing, it was clear they were driven by a desire to help others. One of them was already studying nursing. Linh's girlfriend wanted to be a nurse but her visa was about to expire and she did not think she would be able to afford to stay. You could hear the disappointment in her voice when she explained her circumstances and that it was likely she would have to leave the United States. Jolene wished there was a way she could help her. The other young man did not know yet exactly what he wanted to do.

Listening to their stories and hearing about the challenges they faced and the way that they had overcome so many obstacles already, Jolene encouraged them not to give up on their dreams, even with the difficulties they faced. Once again she was prompted by the Spirit of God. This time, she was being nudged to share her own story and the challenges she had faced and overcome pursuing her own dreams.

Jolene shared with the young people about her detached retina and how it seriously threatened her dream of finishing her seminary education. The surgeries, not being able to see, and not knowing if she would ever regain her sight sufficiently to return to school had been very discouraging for her. She explained that she ended up being out of school for a full year. Then, when she returned she discovered that her eye sight was not good enough to take the required Hebrew classes necessary to finish her degree. All those tiny vowel points in Hebrew were beyond the capacity of her post-surgery vision. Jolene was honest with them. She told them she was very discouraged, but she did not give up. Jolene changed her degree program to one that did not require Hebrew. However, this meant that she had to adjust another part of her dream. She was in the formal process to be ordained as a pastor in the Presbyterian Church USA. She shared with the young people, that in her heart, she believed and knew that the God she served would find some way for her to realize her dream of serving others. She, too, wanted to help others, not medically, but spiritually. Jolene told the dinner guests that after many stops and turns she finally finished her seminary degree in 2010 two years after surgery. Yet, her dream remained on hold for awhile longer.

For three years Jolene served a local congregation as an administrative assistant. This was not her dream, but it did help her learn more about people's faith and ways of helping them. What at first seemed like a detour—a delay in her dream—was actually more of her education to accomplish her dream. Through a variety of circumstances that Jolene never anticipated, during this time she entered a Clinical Pastoral Education program and finished it in 2015. She became a chaplain serving a couple different hospitals in Southern California and then was hired as a hospice chaplain. Her dream was finally realized. Through chaplaincy and hospice work she was helping people with all kinds of medical challenges to understand and explore how their faith was involved in these hard times. She was helping them spiritually and her own experience of a detached retina and the resulting vision impairment, she could now see clearly as an important part of her preparation for helping others. What seemed like obstacles and challenges, had actually equipped her more fully for her career and fulfilling her dream. Even with all the challenges and all the delays, Jolene ended up exactly where she wanted to be—helping people grow through faith. Jolene ended her story by once again, encouraging these young people, no matter what, not to give up on their dreams. She could see on their faces and hear in their voices that they were encouraged by her story. The truth of the matter was, so was she! Who was hosting who on this night?

The shared meal and conversation had gone on well into the night. Jolene and Mike and all the guests got up from the patio table and began to clear it. They all worked together to clean up the dishes and kitchen. Once again, by everyone's active participation, it was hard to tell who was hosting who.

The night's final story was written in the living room with Mike playing the piano and everyone singing songs that were at least somewhat familiar to all. The food, the conversation, and the music created yet another space, a story, so rich in connection that the memory of it would linger for a very long time. When it was finally time for the guests to leave, there were lots of hugs, laughter, and goodbyes in different languages. As the guests got into their cars and drove away, Jolene was in awe of this third space that had been created almost without her planning it at all.

Like Zacchaeus, when the day began, Jolene did not know she would host strangers in her home that night. And, like Zaccheaus, she did not know that, in some way, her guests would end up hosting her. Above all, Jolene had the sense that the conversation around faith was hosted by someone else entirely. Jesus Christ was present in and through Jolene's story and she is confident that same presence will continue through her or others that follow Christ into these spaces and in the lives of these young people. Anyone who is open to giving and receiving hospitality can help to create third spaces where the love and mercy of God can be proclaimed through sharing food, faith, and stories of challenge and encouragement.

But in your hearts revere Christ as Lord.
Always be prepared to give an answer to
everyone who asks you to give the reason
for the hope that you have. But do this with
gentleness and respect.

1 Peter 3:15

Even In Japan

I created the experience. I wrote the curriculum. I edited it several times. In two and a half years I had now personally led six groups through this discipleship experience called *Groundings* and trained twelve other individuals to lead. More than one hundred individuals had been a part of the *Groundings* Experience. In *Groundings,* we learn from Jesus' encounters with people in the Gospels, and then we pay attention to people around us. Jesus by his Spirit continues to encounter people every moment of every day. It's about paying attention and being willing to do and say the kinds of things Jesus did and said. In fact, Jesus said that we would do "even greater things that He did" (John 12:24). My journal is filled with examples, some successful, some failed, of noticing Jesus at work encountering people in everyday places. My call as a disciple is to ask questions, listen, and discern what, if any, role I am to play in what God is doing in these places. These encounters come in the most surprising and unexpected ways.

I was in between the fourth and fifth session of an active *Groundings* group. In a most unexpected way, I received an invitation to go to Japan. The invitation came only two weeks before the trip would take place. And, though there was some possibility of reimbursement, there was no guarantee, and it would cost a chunk of change. I had only forty-eight hours to reply. After a brief conversation with my husband (he is used to my doing things like this) and the enthusiastic support of the head of staff at the church I serve, I said, "yes" to the invitation. Within five hours my flight was reserved. My schedule was rearranged. I could not believe it. I was going to Japan. It was so unexpected. It seemed impossible. Here's why.

My father was a prisoner of war in the Philippine Islands and Japan for three and a half years in World War II. He, like many others, survived the Bataan Death March, two concentration camps, and an animal like transport in the hold of a Japanese cargo ship (called "Hell Ships") to a copper mine in northern Japan owned by Mitsubishi where he was forced to labor for more than a year under inhumane conditions. By the time the war ended and the POW's were liberated, he was near death, weighing barely ninety pounds.

Now, seventy-five years later, Mitsubishi Materials, a successor company to the one that profited from his forced labor was for the first time publicly acknowledging what they had done. Mitsubishi Materials had made and was installing four plaques in four different locations where forced labor was used in WWII. The plaques unequivocally took responsibility and apologized for their treatment. But only one of these plaques was being publicly unveiled and dedicated—the plaque at a mine in Akita, the northernmost prefecture of Japan. This is the mine where my father was forced to labor. Now, I was invited to attend this historic event.

My father died in 2006. For the last six years, I have been a member of the American Defenders of Bataan and Corregidor Memorial Society (ADBCMS). It is an organization that seeks to continue to tell the story and work for education and reconciliation related to the American POW experience in Japan during WWII. The ADBCMS had emailed me that morning and invited me, along with only one other descendant, to attend the unveiling of this plaque at the site of the copper mine where our fathers had been forced to labor and almost died. This was not only an indescribably monumental personal moment, this was an unprecedented historic event. For the first time ever, after seventy-five years, a commercial entity in Japan was taking public and permanent responsibility for the horrific treatment of American and Allied POW's during WWII. How could I *not* go to this event?

Besides the advocacy and educational and diplomatic work of the descendant's group, two Japanese people were the movers and shakers behind this invitation and event. Kinue Tokudome, a Japanese scholar and journalist, had been working for years on educating the Japanese people and lobbying and advocating for telling the truth about the Japanese part in the POW experience in WWII.

She has worked tirelessly to bring Americans and Japanese people together for better understanding and for the hope of a better future. Her website (www.us-japandialogueonpows.org) is an extraordinary educational tool. In addition, she has been actively lobbying Japanese companies who profited from this slave-labor for years, encouraging them to acknowledge the truth about WWII Japanese prisoners of war and how they were treated.

Mr. Yukio Okamoto, a former executive of Mitsubishi Materials, now a board member had also been working for ten years to get his company to own this part of their history. A highly esteemed businessman and historical scholar who lectures on college campuses in Japan and the United States, he had collaborated with others in the company to make this historic unveiling of the plaques at four mines a reality. Mr. Okamoto could not be at the unveiling ceremony. But he had invited me, the other descendant, and Kinue to have breakfast with him the next morning to give him a report on the event.

I was greatly honored by his invitation to breakfast, and honestly, I felt a bit out of my league. The other descendant was a military history scholar. Three scholars and a Presbyterian discipleship pastor around the table. I imagined I would mostly listen, describe my own personal experience at the unveiling and express my gratitude for Mr. Okamoto making all this possible. I never in a million years expected this breakfast to be a *Groundings* experience. All the design and development and teaching and mentoring of the principles of *Groundings* somehow were set aside when I embarked on this trip. After all, there were so many barriers to such a conversation. There would be the social status barrier, the degree of scholarly work barrier, not to mention the language and huge cultural barrier. And Japan is only 1% Christian. The sensitivities of this historic event were fraught with potential offense. It never entered my heart or mind that that breakfast space would become a third space. That this very influential and imposing businessman would open up a conversation about spiritual things with me.

It was a lovely hotel and a splendid breakfast. There was the expected polite banter around the table. Common courtesies were expressed. Kinue and Mr. Okamoto were both fluent in English making the conversation very easy. Mr. Okamoto and Jim Nelson, the other descendant, had met one other time. In fact, when they first met in July 2015, it was Jim's suggestion to Mr. Okamoto that Mitsubishi might do something to commemorate the POW's who were forced to labor in the mine. Mr. Okamoto took the suggestion seriously and that resulted in four plaques being placed at four different facilities and one plaque being publicly unveiled. Now Mr. Okamoto wanted to know how the dedication ceremony at the mine went and how we felt about it. This conversation I expected.

But Mr. Okamoto was thinking deeply and contemplating other things. Gradually the conversation evolved from historical data and events to his own personal struggle with understanding how his people could do such inhumane things. This man was asking questions about human evil. He was trying to understand his own responsibility and trying to find a way that he might contribute to a different future.

Some thoughts that Mr. Okamoto told us that day I will not write about out of respect and care for his continuing journey. What I can tell you, is that this man was doing some serious spiritual wrestling. He was wondering if somehow Japanese people were in some way more predisposed to such evil. He was struggling with taking responsibility for the history of what the Japanese military did to prisoners of war during WWII. His work to apologize to the POW's and to place the commemorative plaques at the four mine locations was all a part of his personal struggle to come to grips with this part of Japanese history and to do something that would demonstrate a different kind of Japanese character.

I was listening carefully and taking in every word. I could tell by the look on his face and by the halting and careful choice of words that Mr. Okamoto was going beyond historical and military or political conversation and even beyond psycho-social musings. He was thinking spiritually—the nature of the human condition and its possibility for good or evil. This conversation was now entering my area of expertise. I still felt totally out of my league to say anything. But as Mr. Okamoto talked, he was increasingly making more and more eye contact with me almost as if he were looking to me to respond. He looked right at me and said, "I am not a religious person but I wonder about these things." Suddenly I knew. This was my "cue." This moment was a *Groundings* experience. This breakfast table was a place where God was at work and I was in a third space, a sacred space, listening to this man describe spiritual musings without the theological or biblical language that we often expect.

Feeling helpless, I gasped a prayer silently. "Lord, help me, I did not come expecting to talk with this man about spiritual things. I do not want to offend or overstep my bounds. But I think you want me to say something. Give me the right words."

Slowly, I responded. I told Mr. Okamoto that I did not have a direct answer to his question, but rather a question and an observation. First the question. I told him that in my faith tradition, Christianity, we believe that we answer to a higher power for what we do or do not do. We believe that all people are capable of inhumane acts. We also believe that we do not answer to our parents, or a President or military leaders. We believe that ultimately, we will answer to God. Knowing we will give an account to God, puts boundaries around what we do. I told him that I had read and understood some to say that the Japanese people, including the military personnel, believed the Japanese Emperor to be divine—God. I asked Mr. Okamoto if, it was possible that the Japanese soldiers believed they were doing God's bidding, following God's orders, not directly but through the military leaders. He did not know for sure but felt that the Emperor did hold significant responsibility for what happened. He explained that though the Emperor did not directly order the treatment of POW's, he believed the Emperor could have stopped it.

Then I told Mr. Okamoto my observation. And this was the most *Groundings*-like moment of all. I told him how very much I admired him and what he was doing and had been doing for years. He had taken and continued to take a lot of public criticism and encountered great resistance for the reconciliation work he was doing. I told him that as I listened to him, I believed that what he was doing *was* religious work because he was doing the kinds of things Jesus did, which are written about in the Gospel accounts of Jesus' life. Jesus also took a lot of criticism from the religious and political leaders of his time. They did not like what he was doing. I also told Mr. Okamoto what Jesus said about religious people. I told him Jesus actually said that he did not come for the religious but for sinners. I finished by reinforcing that I believed he was engaged in religious work, the kind Jesus would do.

As I explained this to Mr. Okamoto I could see the agony on his face release a little. I think a partial smile came across his face for a time. He at least was amused by what I was saying, if not relieved. Since I had entered holy ground and it seemed welcome, I forged ahead. I told him that the Japanese did not have a market on this kind of evil. American history is fraught with it. I told him about the early American history and the treatment of the Native Americans. I described how the experience for them was not a discovery, but an invasion. Their way of life and their place of life was ravaged by the "discovery." White European settlers claimed "Manifest Destiny" to do whatever was necessary to claim the North American continent from sea to sea for God and King. This mentality resulted in genocide of the Native American population. Hundreds of thousands were killed by military action, alcohol infusion, and intentional exposure to smallpox and other diseases the Native Americans had no immunity to fight. Anthropologists estimate that the population was reduced from several million to less than 200,000 before it was over. And to this day the Native Americans are still dealing with the devastating aftermath of that history. No, I told him, the Japanese are not uniquely capable of this kind of evil.

But owning this history, and working to understand it and acknowledge it can lead to a different future. This is holy work. This is the kind of work Jesus did. In my view, this Japanese businessman was describing God at work in and through his life. I was in awe that I was able to be in this place to give witness to it. This was definitely a *Groundings* moment. After creating and teaching the principles for over two years, I had come to Japan with no expectation of seeing God at work in this place. I had no expectation of an invitation to breakfast becoming a third space where Christ was the host. I had no expectation of a Jesus-centered conversation with a prominent businessman in a country where only 1% of the population is Christian. But even there, God is at work and allowed me to be a very small part of what He is doing.

I am still learning. I have taught and preached for years, that God is at work in every square inch of the universe. I had repeated many times the words of the Archbishop of Canterbury, Rowan Williams. In his book, *Tokens of Trust*, he says that whenever we encounter another person we must remember that

God has already encountered that person before we ever arrived. Oh, how Mr. Okamoto reinforced this truth for me. He is in the midst of an active encounter with the living Christ. I do not know how the rest of the story will go, but I give thanks and praise to the Lord that I got to hear and see part of it. Day by day, with God's help I am more open to noticing God at work around me. Week by week I am learning to listen and ask questions about what people are thinking and feeling so that I might see God at work and help them see it, too. More and more I am aware that I do not need to be anxious about what to say or worry about having the "right answers." Listening and learning about other's life experience always opens doors to spiritual conversations. God is at work even in Japan. What a spiritual shot in the arm it was to be there and see it first hand.

Jesus looked at them and said, "With man this is impossible, but not with God; all things are possible with God."
Mark 10:27

Wrapping it Up

The *Groundings* experience is all about following the example of Jesus. He encountered ordinary people in everyday life and invited and engaged them in spiritually consequential conversations. Extraordinary things happened. The socially and morally shunned woman who washed Jesus' feet, became an evangelist. When Jesus encountered her, He used their conversation and her ministry of love and generosity to proclaim the good news of the Gospel. The shunned woman became a teacher of religious leaders. Two thousand years later we are still being taught by her. We are still telling her story just as Jesus said we would be (Matthew 26:13).

The *Groundings* experience is all about noticing God at work all around us. Like the socially and spiritually outcast woman at the well, Jesus engaged with her about who she was and where she was and what she was doing. A well, the need for water, and a string of unsuccessful love affairs opened this woman up to a conversation about worship and grace and the knowledge and love of God. The disciples of Jesus at first only noticed Jesus was talking to a Samaritan woman. But by the time she ran home and came back with a crowd of people to hear this person she believed might be the promised Messiah, the disciples began to notice that God was actually at work in this most unexpected place—the life of an outcast Samaritan woman.

Groundings is also about neighborliness. Jesus through the story of the Good Samaritan did so much more than teach his disciples *who* was their neighbor. He shocked their socks off by using a despised Samaritan as the person in the story who most acted *like a neighbor.* The world is our neighborhood and neighborliness knows no racial, socio-economic, religious, or other predetermined boundaries. We must always be alert to someone who needs a good neighbor, and we must always be willing to be interrupted to act like a neighbor toward someone else. Someone we least expect might be the mission field—or the missionary for the Good News.

A fourth major example of Jesus that is explored in *Groundings* is hospitality. In Jesus' way of encountering people no matter where it happened and what the circumstances were, Jesus became the host in whatever space He entered. Even when He invited himself to the home of Zacchaeus, where it would seem that Zacchaeus is the host, Jesus turns the tables and is the one offering food for eternity. This hospitality is also seen with the woman at the well. Jesus needed a drink but offered her water that would quench her thirst forever. Jesus was hungry and Zacchaeus provided a meal but Jesus offered him spiritual food that radically transformed his life. This is what we mean by third spaces. A driveway, a bird bath in the woods, a restaurant in Tokyo, a sidewalk, a train station, a military base office, the internet—all of these can become places and spaces where we listen to people's story and can notice God at work and in creative and compassionate ways proclaim the Good News of the Gospel. Jesus' example teaches us that both offering hospitality (welcoming the shunned woman into Simeon's house) and receiving it (Jesus inviting himself to the house of Zacchaeus) can provide this kind of space for spiritual transformation.

Finally, *Groundings* is all about the mission of God. In every story Jesus tells, the centerpiece is the mission of God to reconcile the world to himself. We know the verse so well I fear we are dulled to its force and power. John 3:16, "For God so loved the world that He gave His only begotten Son that whosever believes in Him will not perish but have eternal life." Jesus' encounter with Nicodemus reveals that the mission of God brought Jesus into the world. The mission of God sent Jesus to the cross. The mission of God offers eternal life to whoever believes this Good News. Whether He encounters an educated religious leader or a despised outcast woman, Jesus offers the same Good News.

This is what it means to be a disciple and follow Jesus into the world and do the things that Jesus would do and even greater things. It means noticing God at work, proclaiming the Good news, being a good neighbor to all we encounter, giving and receiving hospitality as an opportunity to create a third space for spiritual transformation to take place. Finally, it means we are all about the mission of God every day in every way. We are God's ambassadors as though God were speaking through us (2 Corinthians 5:16). In every encounter with every person in some way, when we offer ourselves, the encounter can be used by God to draw men and women, boys and girls, from every walk and talk of life into the transforming grace and love of God. This love and grace are given in the person and work of Christ through the power of the Spirit at work in each of us in every square inch of the universe.

About the Author

Candie Blankman has been in ministry more than thirty years and an ordained Presbyterian pastor since1996. Candie serves as Pastor of Discipleship, Care, and Engagement at San Clemente Presbyterian Church. Candie has also been a junior and senior high school teacher, a restaurant manager, and has spoken at retreats and conferences for many years, and has been a presenter and coach for SCORRE Speaker Training since 1985. However, Candie's passion is studying the Bible and then teaching and preaching it in a way that reveals the living and powerful Christ.

In 2013 Candie began developing Groundings as a foundational discipleship experience designed to transform the often-complacent church culture from one of knowing about Jesus, to one that is following the living Christ into the world. Through five Jesus narratives, Groundings inspires participants to experience discipleship and evangelism as a seamless garment.

When spare time shows up, she walks the beach and writes and paints. She has been married for 42 years to Drew, an academic editor for InterVarsity Press, and together they have raised three children—this is where she has learned the most about being a minister. Now her five grandchildren are teaching her even more.

Endnotes

1 Anne Naffziger, "Was it Martha's sister Mary or Mary Magdalene who washed Jesus' feet with her tears and dried them with her hair?" busted halo (blog), http://bustedhalo.com/questionbox/was-it-martha%e2%80%99s-sister-mary-or-mary-magdalene-who-washed-jesus%e2%80%99-feet-with-her-tears-and-dried-them-with-her-hair, August 12, 2011.

2 Rowan Williams, *Tokens of Trust* (Louisville, KY: Westminster John Knox, 2007), 35.

3 http://www.pewinternet.org/2015/05/20/americans-attitudes-about-privacy-security-and-surveillance/

4 A foody website isn't so sure about the healthy part and described the salad as, "a pile of iceberg lettuce, a mound of chicken chunks, and a pinch of half-frozen shredded cheese into a big plastic bowl with a lil' cup of Caesar dressing." https://www.thrillist.com

5 http://www.y-malawi.org/

https://www.rippleafrica.org/a-charity-in-malawi-africa/malawi-facts-and-figures

6 "The Hound of Heaven." A poem by Francis Thompson, https://en.wikipedia.org/wiki/The_Hound_of_Heaven.

7 Barbara Brown Taylor, *Gospel Medicine* (Lanham, MD: Rowan & Littlefield, 1995), 85.